ALL IS NUMBER

MEET THE PERSONA OF NUMBERS 1 TO 13

BY MILENA

M PUBLISHING

CONTENTS

ALL IS NUMBER 4
THIRTEEN STORY 14
ENDNOTES 85
BIBLIOGRAPHY 93

ALL IS NUMBER

SOUNDING ETERNAL MUSIC 5
NUMBERS WILL TELL US 5
EACH NUMBER HAS A DISTINCTIVE PERSONALITY 7
FIGURATE NUMBERS 7
INFLUENCE OF NUMBERS 9
TOOL FOR EVERY ANALYSIS 9
WHO SENDS US BIRTHDAY CARDS 10
GAME OF CODES AND MASTER NUMBERS 11

SOUNDING ETERNAL MUSIC

The entirety of Creation is a constantly evolving organism. Its inherent unity is geometrically explainable: no matter how deep into Creation we dive, any given form of it relates to some earlier stages of geometrical evolvement of the primordial One. Smaller patterns are interlaced within the bigger ones, contributing to the intricacy and the richness of the *All That Is*.

The melody of unfolding geometric forms throughout Creation is God's sounding His eternal music.

NUMBERS WILL TELL US

The numbers One, Two and Three are symbols of the basic principles of which natural things consist.

Johannes Kepler[1-1]

There are many kinds of numbers identified, named and classified by those who, in search of a deeper understanding, enjoyed the process of abstraction while pondering various phenomena. The true nature of numbers reveals the integrity, substance and the archetypal significance they possess. Numbers are carriers of essential meanings. They are in the foundation of all sciences and knowledge, and like a bridge they connect Spirit and matter. Numbers define the essence of shapes while geometry reveals them. Moreover, the world of form attributes them with physicality and introduces them to us in line with their purpose.

Studying individual properties of numbers and their connections, as well as their concealed presence in geometry, sheds more light on the great mystery of life and Creation.

2500 years ago, with an understanding that the manifest was the result of numerical combinations, **Pythagoras**[1-2] exclaimed: *All is number!*. Certainly, the world is permeated by numbers. Every sound, as well as every shape, carries them within.

The Pythagoreans believed the power of numbers was perfectly illustrated by a glyph which they used as a sacred symbol of their school. It was a *tetraktys* (Fig. 1.1) comprising four levels of pebbles/dots arranged in an equilateral triangle – starting with one dot at the top level, followed by two on the second level, then three on the third level and four on the fourth, base level.

PYTHAGOREAN BROTHERHOOD

Some beliefs:

- reality is mathematical in its deepest level
- philosophy can be used for spiritual purification
- the soul can achieve union with the divine

Some social norms:

- all members of the brotherhood should be loyal and work in secrecy
- vegetarianism is desirable
- mathematical discoveries and properties are communal
- men and women are regarded as equal
- do not to pick up what has fallen
- avoid busy roads and walk on paths

Many of the Pythagorean rules were metaphorical expressions, truly meaningful only to the initiated. For example, only by being aware that they used black and white beans for voting, can the rule *abstain from beans* acquire its full meaning.

Praise God the Creator who has bestowed upon Man the power to discover the significance of numbers.

Mohammed Mustafa[1-3]
Prophet

Mathematics is the language with which God created the universe. – *Galileo Galilei*[1-4]

The meaning of these dots encapsulated natural philosophy and the finest contemplation of the soul. To an initiate they signified the active and passive nature of numbers, their quality and quantity, and held the truth of numbers being a cause to an effect. However concise it may be, this formation of ten dots contained a great mystery. It is the story of the cosmic unfolding of Creation and dimensions.

● ONE is an idea of the eternal and the absolute. It is the first unity and a metaphor for a definite quantity (One), characterised by an indefinite quality (Many). As a mysterious father-mother of all numbers, it represents an irreducible cause. A qualitative difference between its masculine and feminine potentials perpetuates movement which created Two. In other words, what functioned as a unity of the irreducible One, through the work of its own inner forces, revealed a dualistic nature, and by segregation those properties appeared as *two*.

↔ TWO is a concrete form of One, and a reducible unity. Two exposes the masculine-feminine nature inherited from One and represents a passive state associated with even numbers. The masculine and the feminine, the active and the passive, exist as an inherent nature in everything that is created. A force of Spirit acts between them and links them to each other through mutual action-reaction.

▲ 1.1 – *Tetraktys
is the perennial fountain of the human soul
by which the Pythagorean swore.*
– Johannes Kepler

⟳ The manifestation of Two has brought into existence a new bond made of three units, as a triple power and a model of the stable connection of One with its finite version as Two. The *Holy Trinity*, the most famous unity, is a symbol of this bond and of exceptionally strong concord. As a geometric figure, it is a triangle – the first and the simplest form which requires only three dots to exist. The triangle dwells in all other polygonal forms since they have more than three corners. Any three points in life can be seen as connected by a triangle; thus an endless number of triangular unified fields potentially exist. The entire Creation is woven upon a web of triangles.

The Tao produced the One. The One produced the Two, the Two produced the Three. The Three produced All Things.

Lao Tzu[I-5] (Tao Te Ching)

▲ 1.2 – *Ten balls, the same as four balls, form a tetrahedron*

△ An active nature of One, present within Two, works on the passive nature of Two and as a result it produces THREE. The second triangle illustrates this step and also shows a latent presence of the number Six as a sum of all units in it. So every Three hides a Six within that energy field, the same as every Two hides Three.

△ The next step of Creation manifested FOUR and a third triangle. At that moment a blueprint for the family of Ten was completed and all natures contained in the irreducible one, of the one cycle of Creation, were experienced. The great potential of One realised itself creatively in the causal world and found a new self-expression through Ten.

Movement carries a creative urge while addition and division are two principal ways to Creation. Division, however, assumes existence of a multiplicity since it is the inverse function of multiplication. In its nature, One is attributed with plurality hence it can be viewed as going through a constant division in order to explore its own potential. One could not experience itself through multiplication because one times One always stays the same – One (1x1=1).

Odd numbers are seen as active, creative numbers. The active force of One, working through the passive Two, manifested Three as a solution to the vitality of Two. Three points determine a triangle, defining a plane, which makes Three a metaphor for a *second dimension*. Four points generate a tetrahedron, therefore a *third dimension* was conceptualised by the appearance of Four (Fig. 1.3).

After the emergence of Four, the sum of the numbers becomes Ten (1+2+3+4) and to Pythagoreans it represented all dimensions contained in the universe and consequently the number Ten represented the universe. Ten, actually, was not considered a number but rather a result. One and Two were not believed to be numbers either. They were seen more like parents to the seven numbers of the *Decad*: 3, 4, 5, 6, 7, 8 and 9.

EACH NUMBER HAS A DISTINCTIVE PERSONALITY

For the Pythagoreans, each number had a distinctive personality while belonging to a particular group of numbers emphasised its unique attributes. Outside their numerical family, numbers were also related to certain gods and goddesses, muses, human virtues, planets, musical tones, letters, and many other aspects of life. According to the Pythagoreans, they were ciphers and guides for they were seen as the codes of the cosmic mind in its self-expressing processes. Hence with **Pythagoras** started what we could call the blending of science and religion, of reason and belief. During more than two thousand years, that marriage suffered and experienced its end. We are to revive it now by reconciling logic and intuition, matter and Spirit, heart and mind, in the chambers of spiritual science.

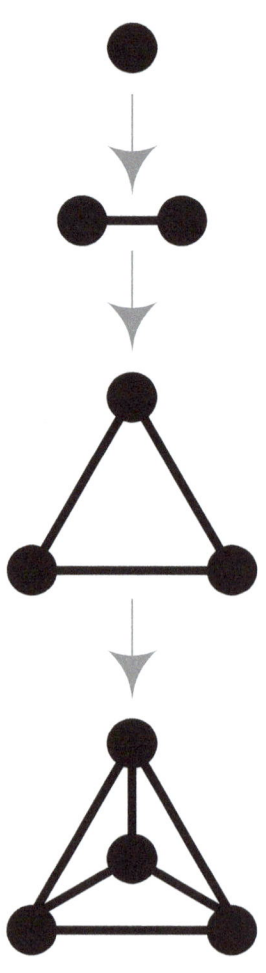

▲ *1.3 – The unfolding of dimensions*

FIGURATE NUMBERS

Figurate numbers are those that can be shown as a regular geometrical figure composed of equally spaced pebbles/points (Fig. 1.5).

Depending on the figure made, these numbers can be *triangular, square, pentagonal,* etc., or spatial: *tetrahedral, cubic, pyramidal,* etc. There are many types of *figurate numbers* and each can be expressed through a mathematical formula.

▲ *1.4 – Star hexagonal numbers are composed of six triangular numbers and one centred hexagonal number (except the number Thirteen)*

All things which can be known have number; for it is not possible that without number anything can be either conceived or known.

Philolaus[I-6]

As we can notice from the illustrations in figure 1.5, these configurations reveal some properties and relations between certain numbers that are not evident in any other way. For example, a very rare property of the number 37 becomes visible: it is both a *star* and a *centred hexagonal number,* and is the only such number lesser than a thousand.

$n(n+1)/2$
Triangular
Numbers:
1, 3, 6, 10, 15…

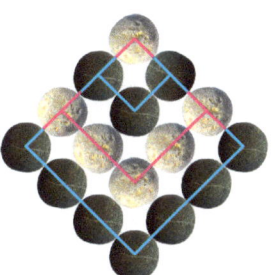

n^2
Square
Numbers:
1, 4, 9, 16, 25…

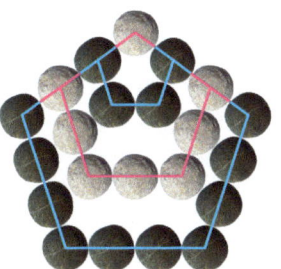

$n(3n-1)/2$
Pentagonal
Numbers:
1, 5, 12, 22, 35…

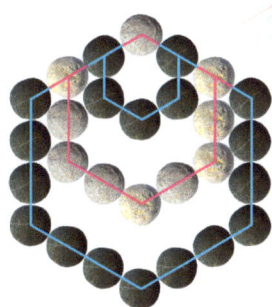

$n(2n-1)$
Hexagonal
Numbers:
1, 6, 15, 28, 45…

$(3n^2-3n+2)/2$
Triangular Pyramidal
Numbers:
1, 4, 10, 19…

$n^2+(n-1)^2$
Square Pyramidal
Numbers:
1, 5, 13, 25…

$(5n^2+5n+2)/2$
Pentagonal Pyramidal
Numbers:
1, 6, 16, 31…

$3n^2-3n+1$
Centred Hexagonal
Numbers:
1, 7, 19, 37…

Star Hexagonal Numbers: $6n(n-1)+1$

13 – star number
7 – centred hexagonal number

37 – star number
19 – centred hexagonal number

73 – star number
37 – centred hexagonal number

▲ 1.5 – *Examples of figurate numbers*

INFLUENCE OF NUMBERS

In numerology, which is a branch of predictive science, every single number within the *Decad* is associated with a planet, so it becomes a cipher of the properties assigned to that particular planet. Thus the planet associated with a given number becomes crucial to the nature of that number.

Numerologists draw our attention to quality as a property of numbers, rather than to the association of numbers with quantities as we are used to making. According to numerology, the influence of a number is represented through many forces, events, states and things. For example, each number from One to Nine is associated with a colour, a gem stone, a metal, an element and a season, and also reflects its influence on health, psyche and physique, taste, parts of the body, general outlook, tendencies and the behaviour of a person. Grouped in families, numbers display friendly, neutral or hostile affinities towards one another. Determining the numbers relevant to a person, numerologists make connection between the attributes of these numbers and the life of the person.

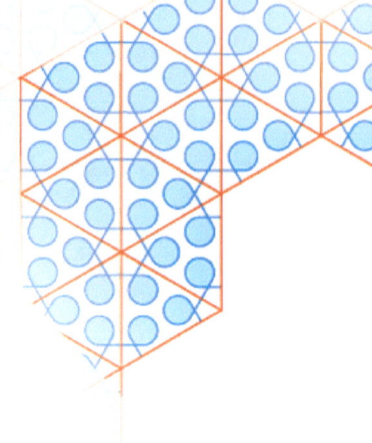

One of the divisions of numbers is into even and odd numbers. For numerologists, these two groups possess opposite qualities. Even numbers are feminine, lunar, alkaline, magnetic and static in their nature while odd numbers are masculine, solar, acidic, electrical and dynamic. Since even numbers are static, the same as the sum of two even or two odd numbers, they are not desirable. The dynamism of odd numbers allows change.

Numerological determination of one's life makes sense only to those who are prepared to see a wider picture of reality within which all is connected. When we step into the world of abstraction with courage and trust in fate, we break through the surface of the superficial and dive into the world of elementary and underlying simplicity. From that point of view, each of us seems to be an epitomised and unique combination of everything that influences everything. We are numerically designed characters within the grand play of the cosmic mind. In the plurality of actors and expressions of that play, the value constants are entrusted to numbers.

TOOL FOR EVERY ANALYSIS

Numbers are part of our life, and they constitute a particular map of it. Their use became evident with the first trading practices where numbers of goods were counted to determine the fairness of exchange. Today, for example, we find numbers on money, pay slips, registration plates, telephone books, statistical reports, identification documents, tickets and calendars. Numbers convey not only the meaning of the quantities but also represent ways of establishing order.

Numbers are the superior tool for every analysis and organisational endeavour. They are behind all structures and strategies. The only precise way to express the property of life called *quantity* is through numbers. A verbal description of quantity

All the calculation You use on the World Planet at the moment can never be compared to or calculated with the calculations belonging to the Dimension-beyond.
...

The value Units of each Dimension change according to numbers in accordance with its Frequency Layers. For example, the calculation 2 x 2 = 4 in Your Dimension, is taken as the square of 4 in another Dimension. And its value Units there is 16.

In another Dimension, 2 is added to this number 16 and there, the value of 2 x 2 is known as 18. In another Dimension, two 7s constitute a Total and thus, number 2 there carries a value of 14.

The Knowledge Book[(1-7)]
(S2, p 1005, par 10;
p 1006, par 4,5)

Philosophy is written in this grand book, the universe, which stands continually open to our gaze. But the book cannot be understood unless one first learns to comprehend the language and read the letters in which it is composed. It is written in the language of mathematics, and its characters are triangles, circles, and other geometric figures, without which it is humanly impossible to understand a single word of it.

Galileo Galilei,
(The Assayer, 1623)

is not accurate enough and not universal, since there are many levels of consciousness and many languages within human societies.

Some cultures like Arabic[I-8], Greek and Jewish[I-9] have assigned a numerical value to each of their letters, which enables them to convert words and sentences into numbers. For that purpose, all three of these alphabets use the so-called *sequential value* (SV) and *numerical value* (NV) systems[I-10].

In the *sequential value system* each letter is given a number sequentially, following the succession of natural numbers from 1, 2, 3, 4,... up to the last letter. So the number reveals the place in the alphabet of the given letter. For example, the letter M is the 13th letter of all three alphabets and Thirteen is the *sequential value* in each one of them. In the *numerical value system,* the numbers also increase as the position of the letter in the alphabetical series gets further from the beginning and the nominal value is always a multiple of ten. For example, the letter T in this system has the following values: in Arabic – 400, in Greek – 300 and in Hebrew – 400[I-10].

Isopsephia and, more recently, *theomatics* are terms used to refer to the study of the alphanumerical relationships within the 24 letters of the Greek alphabet. Hebrew has 22 basic letters (5 of them have a different value when positioned as the last letter in a word) and its alphanumerical system is called *gematria*.

The alphabetic numbering systems manage to bridge the verbal and the numerical worlds, thus thinning the veil between them. They are ancient: there is evidence of their use in Greece which goes as far back as the 5th century BC, and the 2nd century BC in Israel. For more than two millennia these systems have facilitated the study of the holy scriptures in search of their hidden codes and special meanings. This practice reveals how at some level the ancients understood that the supreme source speaks one language (numerical) but in different cultures it uses different letters (letter frequencies) to convey the same meanings. Learning words and languages is a matter of training however, meaning is acquired parallel to the growth of our consciousness.

WHO SENDS US BIRTHDAY CARDS

The role numbers play in our lives is unique and indispensable. Each year when celebrating our birthday, we express our appreciation of numbers; in particular of the numerical combination that is us. This custom is based on a profound understanding of life and on a positive and joyful attitude to it. Each new cycle of self-resonance is marked by a number from a procession of numbers that our life can be seen as. Birthday cards are a pleasant reminder of the significance of numbers. They are sent by the Creator, who signs them using the hand of our dear ones.

However universally understood it may be, the language of numbers remains mysterious and magical like music. It is in the basis of coding systems and as such defines everything – from our DNA to vast physical realities.

Our reality is an integral part of a far bigger structure within *All That Is*. We reside in one of its universes. The secret of our universe is also our secret. The entire universe is a unified macro-atomic formation regulated by the same numbers and laws as the micro-atomic constitution of our body. This is the reason we can feel God.

GAME OF CODES AND MASTER NUMBERS

Human being of our planet is capable of accessing only a particular visual segment of *All That Is* and a divinely determined level of information/knowledge of higher realms. That portion depends on our evolution. The measure of human evolutionary evolvement is in the power (frequency/speed) of our thought to reach and attract higher energy layers (new information). Our evolutionary evolvement is also indicated by our level of consciousness – which guides us through all perceptions and cognitions be they mental, visual or emotional. In a high level of consciousness, the period from becoming aware of a challenge through getting an idea/solution and the necessary action is short. However, intellect and logic of the heart are not to be bypassed.

$$111 = 37 \times 3 \times 1$$
$$222 = 37 \times 3 \times 2$$
$$333 = 37 \times 3 \times 3$$
$$444 = 37 \times 3 \times 4$$
$$555 = 37 \times 3 \times 5$$
$$666 = 37 \times 3 \times 6$$
$$777 = 37 \times 3 \times 7$$
$$888 = 37 \times 3 \times 8$$
$$999 = 37 \times 3 \times 9$$

▲ *1.6 – This series of 3-digit master numbers reveals a regularity in appearing of the number 37 in them (Fig 2.6.12).*

*Alphanumerical studies of **The Bible** show an ample presence of the number 37.*

The essence and vibrations of numerical equations are within your soul signature… You are a numerical encoding within the flesh. Every organ, every drop of blood, every atom in your body can be explained numerically. You are in an equation of evolutionary proportion that everyday re-defines itself and re-evaluates what it is on that day. For you are never the same components two days in a row.

All thoughts can be explained numerically. All longings can be explained and exclaimed numerically.

Gillian MacBeth-Louthan[I-11]
(Quantum Newsletter)

As our consciousness expands, numbers might reveal some of their other attributes to us. Soon, we could, for example, discover that numbers also hold some time-determining qualities, indicating past, present or future, relative to the context they appear in. To add to our approach to numbers, *The Knowledge Book* reveals that, in some other realities, the results of numerical calculations give different values to ours, due to the impact of the dimensional frequencies in which calculations take place (see page 24).

The group of numbers called *master numbers* holds some unusual qualities we are yet to explore fully. Such numbers consist of two or more of the same digit and thus illustrate the basic creational principle of reflection/symmetry. Energetically they emphasise the meaning of the single digit they originate from and, at the same time, define its new qualitative level.

Emanated into the ether as joined energies, viewed from a mathematical perspective, our thoughts produce some numerical combinations. All numbers are powerful carriers of information. The frequencies they hold, when harmonised in the form of *master numbers*, can represent particular things, situations, places or beings and originate from the electromagnetic frequencies of our thoughts. *Master numbers* record essential energetic signatures of phenomena and then serve as recipes for producing the same outcomes elsewhere. They mark an exceptional quality of multidimensional value, therefore the information they store is highly applicable in multiple realities.

What would be the numerical combination of our collective dream of heaven on Earth? We are all together contributing to it by raising our awareness and consciously transmuting the lower energies of fear, negativity and struggle into compassion, love and creativity. Once we realise the ultimate purpose of our life on Earth, and fulfil our collective dream, its mathematical formula will be our gift to other worlds to apply it and see their dreams come true.

Ἰησους

Alphanumerical analysis of the words *Allah* and *Jesus* reveals that their numerical value is a so-called *master number*:
66 – ALLAH (in Arabic)
888 – JESUS (in Greek)[II-8]

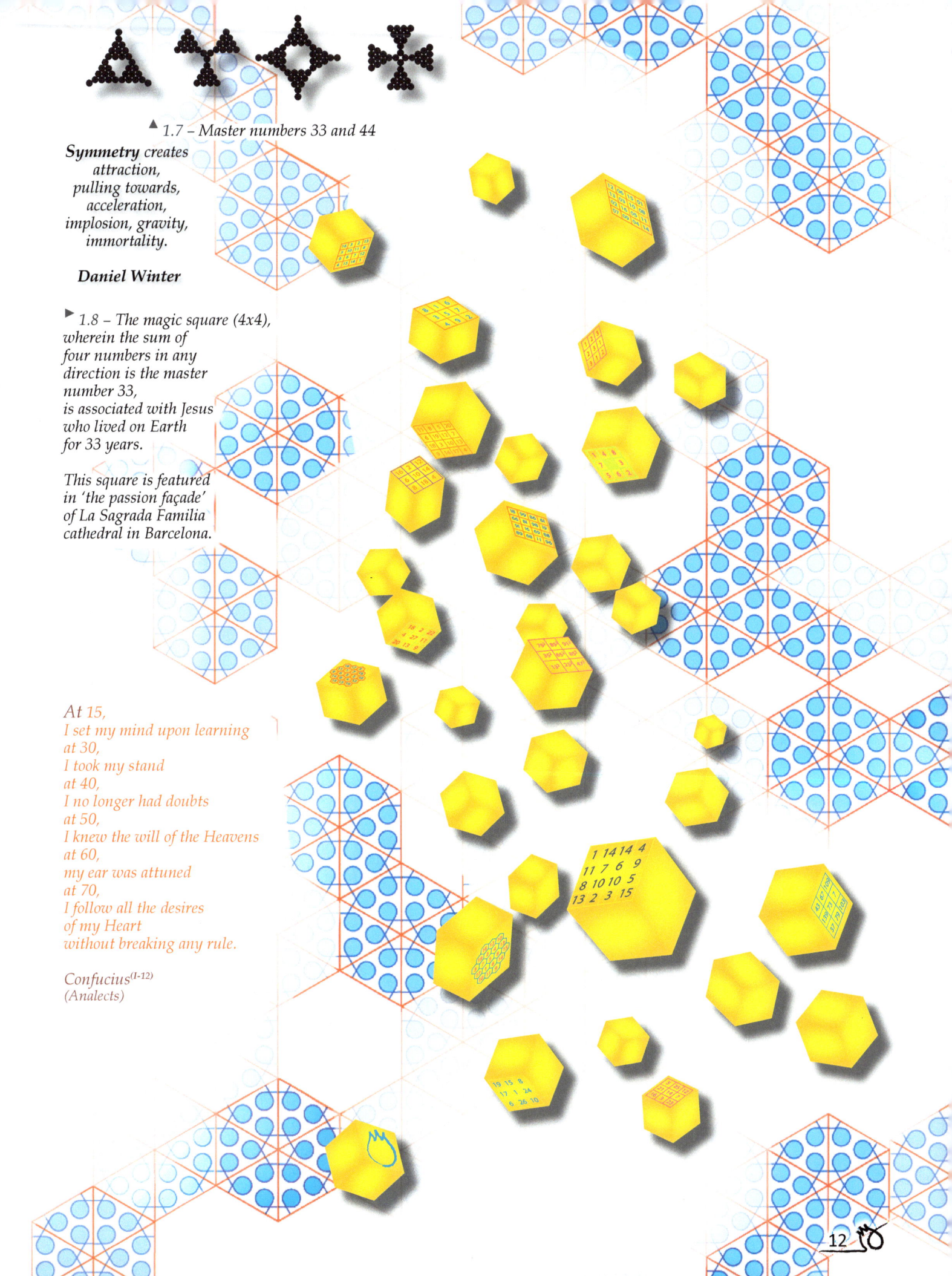

▲ 1.7 – Master numbers 33 and 44

Symmetry creates attraction, pulling towards, acceleration, implosion, gravity, immortality.

Daniel Winter

▶ 1.8 – The magic square (4x4), wherein the sum of four numbers in any direction is the master number 33, is associated with Jesus who lived on Earth for 33 years.

This square is featured in 'the passion façade' of La Sagrada Familia cathedral in Barcelona.

*At 15,
I set my mind upon learning
at 30,
I took my stand
at 40,
I no longer had doubts
at 50,
I knew the will of the Heavens
at 60,
my ear was attuned
at 70,
I follow all the desires
of my Heart
without breaking any rule.*

Confucius[I-12]
(Analects)

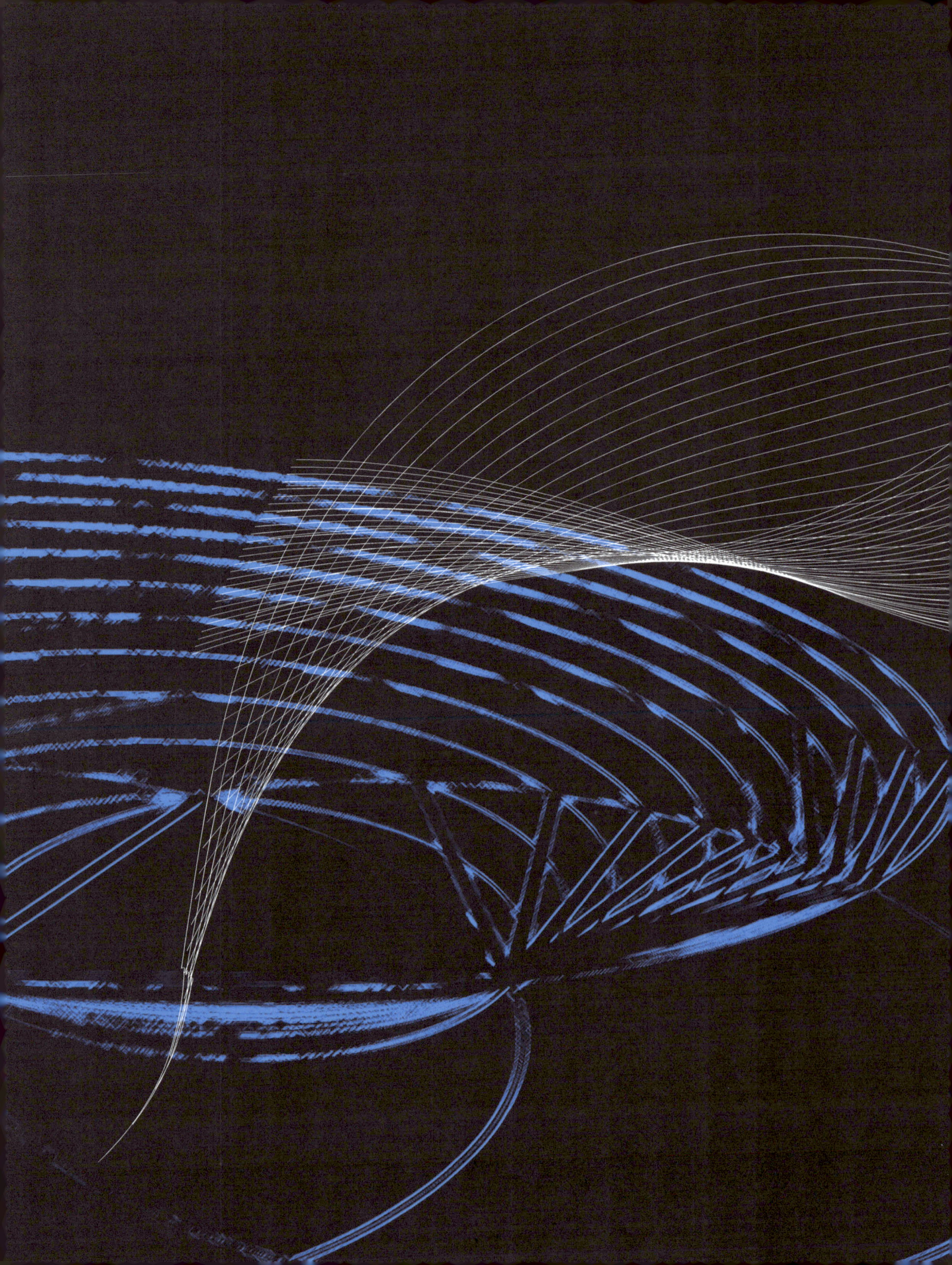

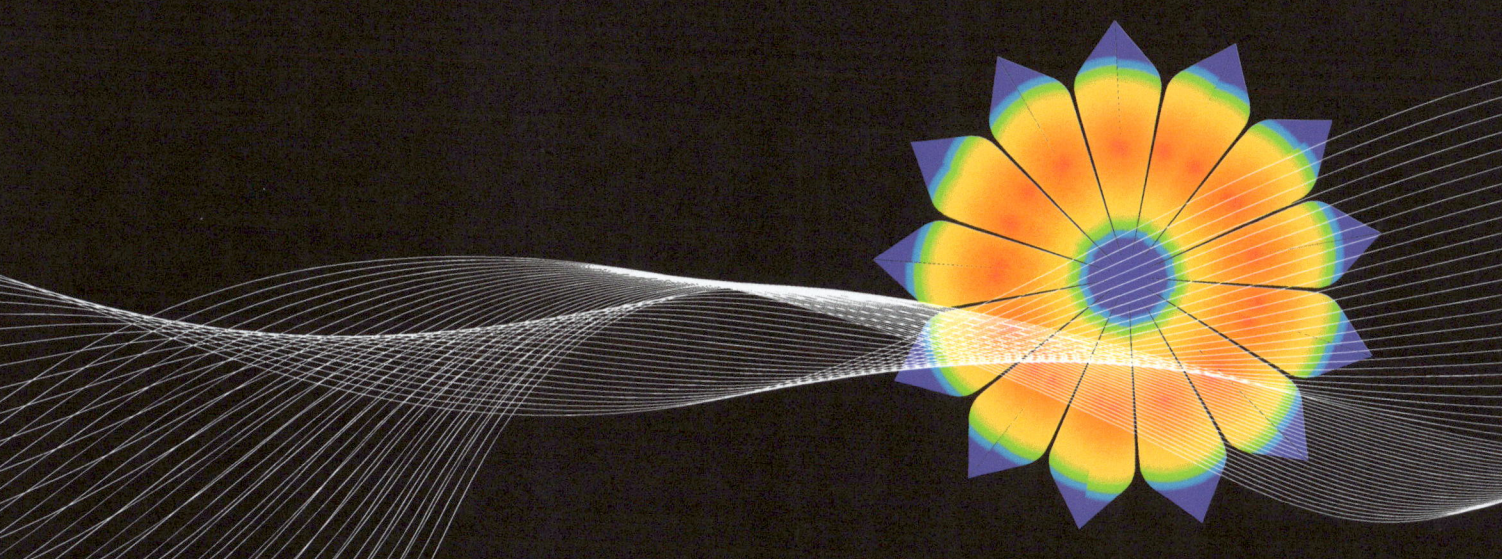

THIRTEEN STORIES

1	15
ONE	15
2, 4, 8	20
TWO	21
FOUR	30
EIGHT	35
3, 6, 9, 12	42
THREE	43
SIX	47
NINE	53
TWELVE	61
5, 10	63
FIVE	64
TEN	68
7, 11, 13	71
SEVEN	72
ELEVEN	79
THIRTEEN	81

ONE

*I, Who Am a Soul in each Flesh, Am a Whole with You.
You, who have taken the Divine Light of Your Spirit from Me,
are Soul, a Flesh, and also Everything.*

*You, who search for Your LORD, are You at that instant.
And You, who try to Attain Yourself, is Me. The one
who Thinks of Me is You and the One Who Thinks of You is Me.*

The Knowledge Book (F36, p 598, par 9,10)

▲ *2.1.1 – Symmetry of numbers 1 to 13. Number 1 is like a parent number present in every other number.*

▲ *2.1.2 – Christ Pantocrator – detail of a mosaic from the Hagia Sophia museum (ex church/mosque) in Istanbul[11-1.1]*

In the presence of His Glory, closely watch your heart so your thoughts won't chain you.

*Mevlana
Celaleddin-i Rumi[11-1.2]*

IRREDUCIBLE ONE

Within the tranquillity of the Great Void, a pregnant point of the unknown power expanded with an equal intensity in all directions and a sphere, or what we call One, appeared.

One is the sole custodian of His own secret. If that were not so, One would not be One. One is responsible for providing life to all that (He/She/It) creates.

Throughout human cultures the sphere and the circle, being its two-dimensional aspect, have been used as geometrical symbols of One, oneness, singularity, wholeness of Creation, unity, God, *Monad*. The One is equally the seed and the fruit of Creation. All came from One, belongs to One and is One.

MOST ECONOMICAL OF ALL GEOMETRIC SHAPES

The sphere (circle), represents the first Creation within the Great Void and is connected to it through an infinite number of points along its circumference. The *irrational number* π (Pi=3.14...), as a godly cipher, holds the memory of that origin and wisdom of shaping the most perfect form.

In comparison to other shapes, the circle encloses the greatest area with the smallest perimeter. This means, for example, that if we have three birthday cakes with the same perimeter, shaped as a circle, square and triangle, and we cut them into an equal number of pieces each, the biggest piece will be one from the round cake.

The same efficiency of round shapes can be observed in case of a dining table. A round one, in comparison to other shapes of the same perimeter, provides the biggest area to be used for more dishes, and to be shared by more people. Similarly, if we use round plates they will hold more food than plates of other shapes of the same perimeter.

Atum is the Whole which contains everything.
He is One, not two.
He is All, not many.
The All is not many separate things,
but the Oneness that subsumes the parts.
The All and the One are identical.
You think that things are many
when you view them separate,
but when you see they are all hung on the One,
and flow from the One,
you will realise they are united –
linked together,
and connected by a chain of Being
from the highest to the lowest,
all subject to the will of Atum.

Thoth[III-1-3]

▼ 2.1.3 – Unknown Potential, reduced to a point, manifested One as a finite self-aspect

You can know yourself as yourself,
and also know yourself as them.
And know that all of us are only One
– God seeing God.

The Messages from God
through Yael and Doug Powell[III-1-1]

DIVINE BUBBLES

The circle is a symbol of the number One. This number represents God and the singularity of His supreme Creation. The mind that thinks linearly associates the number One with the first in a group, with the best. The ancient Greeks did not consider it a number but rather an archetypal parent.

The circle stands for unity, also symbolised through the number One. All Creation is an intricate skein of interdependent components of One. How much we support the coherence of the Total depends on our consciousness level, since it requires placing common interests above individual ones.

We, humans of this planet, still consider untrue or non-existing the things we do not know about or cannot see. At the same time, we tend to believe that all we see is real! That is why the rapid shift in consciousness, which is orchestrated by the *divine plan*, is about opening ourselves to other ways, or realities, that we did not know were possible or existed.

Staying open requires willingness, and assumes readiness, to accept one's own inner changes and to take responsibility for all their consequences. Thus, when we open ourselves to the new, we start seeing things with a different eye which embraces differences perceiving them as the richness of Creation and an advantage rather than a disadvantage. By shifting the focus from physical to metaphysical, from chemistry to alchemy, we gradually stretch our observational perspective, widening our awareness and consciousness. That is our inner path and the way for turning lead into gold; the path of becoming living alchemists who understand the laws of Creation and who consciously apply them.

The circle rotates in every wheel, so it represents continuous flow, inevitable change and equality in facing destiny. It is also a symbol of a cycle.

Since being is a process and processes are cyclic, the circle is inscribed in all life processes of human being, plants, animals, planets, stars, galaxies, or *Gürzes*[II-1.5]. Shorter cycles/events are included in the larger ones, as a day is a part of a week, a week of a month and a month of a year, and so on towards the boundaries beyond which there is no time/energy/existence as we know it.

Noticing cycles is a matter of going deeper enough in our observations. Nevertheless, they are always there – as an endless web of rings that reflects a geometric aspect of life.

There seems to be a very specific energy quality that can be detected when systems are in perfect balance. This energy quality is linked to a source beyond the time-space frame of the system itself. The balancing seems to come from a transcendental source. This can be understood when we take the analogy with the geometry of a circle where the balance of the shape is achieved by the point in its centre.
Dr Ibrahim F. Karim[II-I-6]

VISION GUIDE

As opposed to its circumference, which is a symbol of cyclic motion, the centre of a circle represents its focal point. There would not be a beginning without a focal point, neither would there be any further progress and sustenance without it. The focal point is an invisible point of immense density, power and importance. It is often abstract, belonging to the world of ideas and Spirit from where the manifested is conceived. Hardly any project will come to fruition without the holder of a vision, without someone supplying the nourishment from that inner focal point placed within infinity.

Any point on the circumference of a circle can be seen as a vision guide. It can illustrate the starting place and the target. We begin with a vision and work on it with the passing of time. When the vision from the starting point meets its acceptable outcome, we achieve completion. A circle closes and we arrive at a new beginning.

The point is also a representative of our mental and emotional focus. In any given moment, there is a point where our thoughts converge. We cannot easily avoid a state of being that does not imply thought activity. With meditation it is possible to train ourselves to acquire glimpses of pure awareness beyond the functioning of thoughts. Such an encounter with our timeless self happens at a sacred point found in the sublime stillness of our heart.

The earth was without form and void, and darkness was over the surface of the deep. And the Spirit of God was hovering over the surface of the waters.

The Bible
(Genesis 1:2)

▲ 2.1.4 – *Divine descending*

... and the Spirit of God hovered over the waters – illustration by Milena[II-1.7]

MEETING PLACE

A line is a recorded movement of a point. Out of the countless number of points that make a line, to identify one point on the line, another line needs to cross it. It is a similar case with humans.
A conscious meeting of two human beings is based on their sharing of at least one common point. An infinite number of points which make up our being becomes animated when another bundle of points, that constitutes the infinity of another being, interacts with us on the same coordinates. The meeting point is the opening of a new door to a road with no end. In order for any number of human beings to genuinely meet, there must be a ground of identified common points reached by their visions, needs or feelings.

Since it provides each action with coordinates and directions, *point* is relevant to every movement. The point is also a metaphor for the target, reason, or meaning of all our endeavours.

WHAT IS A POINT

Though visible in geometry, a point is more of an inner-world category than a tangible phenomenon. It is the most abstract of all geometric notions, an exclusive tool of consciousness, and its utmost secret.

The point is a concentrated form of a sphere (circle) and can be seen as the source of an infinite creativity, manifested through the sphere's expanding and contracting rhythms throughout Creation.

> The dot, point, seed or undifferentiated whole, is a container of infinity. It is an utmost condensed state of being poised to transform. In tantric tradition[II-1.8] the point is a power emblem called *bindu* and represents the source of all Creation and a place of origin and of return.

The point reminds us of the abstract side of reality. It is also a category of mind – its ability to concentrate, to focus. As an initial source of the manifest, it symbolises the stillness and infinite potential of the innermost essence. It is magnificent in its enigmatic simplicity. All forms have emerged from the point. It is primeval and ultimate.

A point fulfils its function even without being active. By emanating its own essence only, it provides meaning. The content and power of a point are infinite and beyond comprehension. There is no time when a point does not exist in one way or another. Our life is profusely inhabited by points: they mark events and targets on our life-line.

Intangible while present, points are the Creator's reflection. His grandness can fit into a dimension as minute as a point and thus illustrate His own mysterious power. Only He, the most supreme magician of all, can hide inside the point and then burst out of it, manifesting worlds and galaxies. What a way to spread His might across the Great Void!

And what is the *point* after all if, according to our knowledge, it has no attributes to be described physically?

Point is both a Whole and its smallest particle.

Human Being is a focal point that mirrors the Living Total.

A point is that which has no part.

Euclid

▲ *2.1.5 – God spelling His own name*

▲ *2.1.6 – One petal is enough to make a flower*

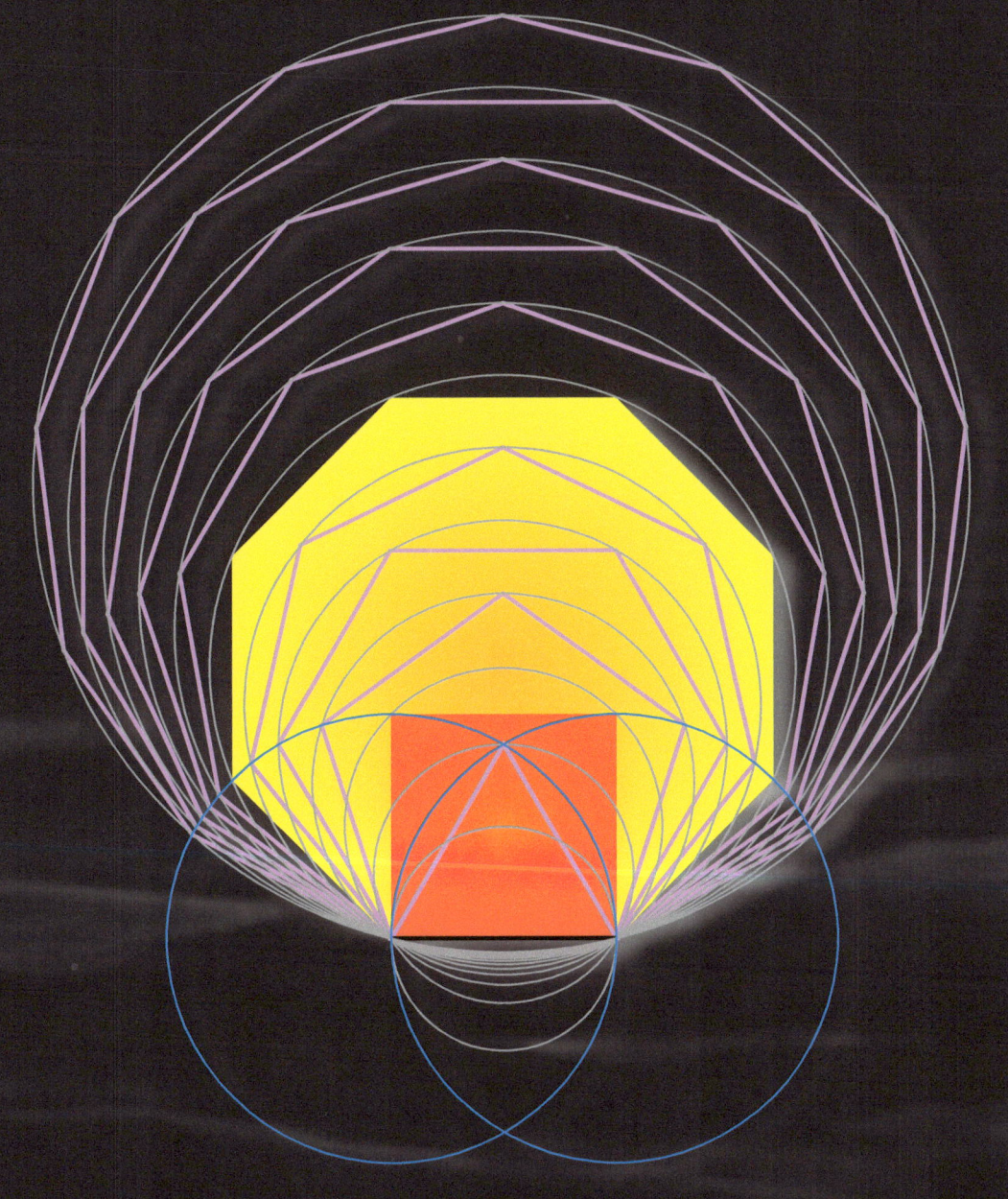

TWO

For where two or three are gathered in my name, there am I among them.
The Bible (Matthew 18:20)

Jesus said to him, I am the way, and the truth, and the life.
No one comes to the Father except through Me.

The Bible
(John 14:6)

▲ 2.2.1 – Number 2, placed in the group with 4 and 8, within the first 13 natural numbers

▼ 2.2.2 – When implicit becomes explicit – vesica pisces

VESICA PISCES

From within the potential of the initial sphere of One, in the process of *Genesis*, another sphere of the same radius emerged with its centre on the surface of the initial sphere. This step produced two overlapping spheres with a common almond-like section. For the Pythagoreans it was a symbol of intersection of the world of the Divine with the world of matter: a mixing bowl of Spirit and a cave of the *Monad*. In the West, it is called the *vesica pisces* (*fish's bladder*, in Latin) while in the East is known as a *mandorla* which means *almond shape* (Fig. 2.2.2). This whole event can be seen as the mirroring of the primordial One, or a particular self-reflection whereupon Two, the *Dyad*, was manifested.

... as you live, if you can adapt to the Philosophy,
"The One Facing You is who You are"
No Education can ever Reach Your Wisdom.
And You discover the Genuine Happiness then.

Vedia Bülent (Önsü) Çorak
(Light)

It is the *Dyad* that emphasises the opposite values present in the *Monad*. Segregated properties of the primordial One create the initial tension between the opposites and a potential for shift. Similar elements are grouped in an almond-shaped area, while different ones are being kept away by a mutual repelling force. So, Two has the ability to attract as well as to repel.

The *Dyad* is a specific outcome of the *Monad*, never the result of a simple addition of One to One because there are no two *Monads*, only ONE. It means that all Creation is an internal process, as a particular division or metamorphosis of the primeval unity. One undergoes transformation so that the implicit becomes explicit, and the new self-expression becomes essentially connected to the previous one. Thus everything created can be traced back to the primal origin.

A *vesica pisces* is a symbol of duality and its resolution. Opposite elements, acting through the *Dyad*, are catalysts of the creative process – in contrast to the sameness which is sufficient in itself. Working with the dark, the light is always ready to transmute conflict into peace and unity, and to further Creation. Thus behind the almond-shaped doors of the *vesica pisces*, plurality is waiting to emerge.

The number Two stands for the polarity where one pole cannot exist without the other. This principle is applicable throughout life. To the ancient Greeks, *Dyad* was a step in Creation that betrayed unity and as such was considered an illusion.

DOT BY DOT

When Two is manifested, the first line appears represented with its segment between the two dots (centres of two spheres). A line is infinite and can signify life-force, or energy movement, behind the shifting of a dot. The line can also be seen as the string of a musical instrument. Since the line does not have real substance, it symbolises a soundless sound of a spiritual realm.

Being is an aspect of non-being; non-being is no different from being. Until you understand this truth, you won't see anything clearly.

Seng Ts'an[II-2.1]

Cause and effect are interchangeable in holistic systems. A frame of mind which entertains hatred, revenge, or resentment, attracts a perpetrator – it must; all energy relationships are subject to advanced physics, and these are some of the programs of nature's computer system.

Dr Noel Huntley[II-2.2]

The very first dot of Creation is still rolling on, while tracing its course on the canvas of life. Whenever it stops temporarily, new lines and shapes emerge as a record of the path it has covered.

Shapes are a construct of lines limited by endpoints. From the first dot's relocation, an infinite display of life forms starts. Writing, sculpting, building, all are a visible record of a moving dot guided by the human mind. Dots and lines in nature, and us as a part of it, are ultimately the Creator's direct expressions. They are units of the Spirit that leaked into the world of the tangible.

◀ 2.2.3 – *Creator sitting on a vesica pisces throne*

MIGHTY I AM PRESENCE

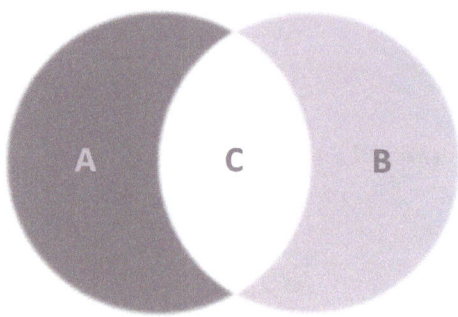

◀ 2.2.4 – Vesica pisces and
I Am That I Am

A = I Am
B = I Am
(virtually mirrored)

A + B + C = I Am That I Am

*God replied to Moses,
'I AM WHO I AM.
This is what you are to say
to the Israelites:
I AM has sent me to you.
...
This is My name forever;
this is how I am to be remembered
in every generation.*

*The Bible
(Exodus 3:14,15)*

Let us assume **I Am** to be One, symbolised by the first sphere. Exploring its own potential, **I Am** mirrored itself by creating 'something to relate to' and thus enabling learning from consequent occurrences. From that moment, assessing all expressions of self as the wholeness of its own Creation, **I Am** could assert: **I Am That I Am**.

I Am is a forever growing self-experience of the Total, through generations of geometrical forms, and a synonym of an omnipresent awareness. Each uttered **I Am** evokes divine presence, echoing throughout the cascades of the Total.

The *sacred geometry* is a vibrational matrix of the deep silence frequencies of the only presence and the only power – mighty **I Am**.

*You created this servant
of Yours and
brought him into being
from a drop of water.
I do not even have the right
to say I love You and yet,
I do love You.*

*I always remember You.
I know that even my
being able to remember You
is also due to Your guidance.*

*My mentioning
Your Name of Majesty
left me dizzy, bewildered,
and amazed.*

*Is it possible
to imagine anyone
in this world loving
the Divinity
and not becoming
intoxicated
with such affection?*

Rabia(II-2.3)
(O My Generous Master!)

▲ 2.2.5 – From the Thought ocean
to the Consciousness ocean...

*Again, I assure you:
If two of you on earth agree
about any matter
that you pray for,
it will be done for you
by My Father in heaven.*

*The Bible
(Matthew 18:19)*

CONSCIOUS EXPERIENTIAL POSSIBILITIES

As a fragment of the *consciousness totality*, our consciousness is endeavouring to understand and realise its own purpose.

When One expresses itself through the *Dyad*, a corresponding consciousness is in function. It is *dualistic consciousness* characterised by a perception of strong opposites, strong polarisation of opinions, feelings and vocabulary. When *dualistic consciousness* dominates, then our divine self, which is beyond polarity as a holder of *unity consciousness,* is either still in a deep sleep or in the process of awakening.

The human brain acts as a template for operational modes of consciousness, wherein the left and right brain hemispheres provide different experiential possibilities.

The perception and functioning of consciousness processed through the left side of the brain are marked by the ability to perform causal, logical and linear thinking, categorising and separating; to display egoism, competitiveness, quantitativeness, to use force (Newtonian laws), and to focus on non-resonant energies. The left side is analytical, mathematical, and keen to examine the details. While working on the basis of facts, within the context of the external world, it is subject to doubt and distrust.

Contrary to the mode of the left brain hemisphere, consciousness processed in the right side of the brain acts by displaying unity, benevolence, cooperation, non-linearity, qualitativeness, quantum laws, subjectivity and acceleration without the use of force, focusing on resonant energies, holistic and artistic attributes, and a strong reference to inner space in search of a broad understanding through intuitive impressions. It uses and stores spiritual experiences and those related to meanings and super-causal order hence it is able to access deeper levels of meanings and acquire new horizons. According to English scientist **Dr Noel Huntley**, separation is always the result of frequencies being out of phase, of energies being non-resonant and non-synchronous, which is the physics behind the left side of the brain's activity and of the reality created by the consciousness processed through it.

And the consciousness of God I Am is everywhere at once. Love perceiving Love, perceiving Love as Itself.

The Messages from God through Yael and Doug Powell

A non-resonant environment is a field where effort, pushing, insisting and conflict are being generated. In functioning through the right side of the brain, resonant, in-phase energies act within a holistic approach. Such consciousness enables one to be in the right place at the right time, thus flowing through experiences effortlessly. Some would call it luck, but it is pure physics. One of humanity's current evolutionary needs is to fully understand the difference between the functional domains of the two brain hemispheres.

▲ *2.2.6 – Levels of focusing. Is there an end to them? No – for as long as we resist all distractions.*

RECOGNITION OF OPPOSITE ELEMENTS

Seeing the common factors in situations of a dualistic nature requires experience and wisdom. Noticing the play of opposites, understanding its purpose and transcending the need to act through *duality consciousness*, takes time. It also takes time to learn that every disharmony holds elements of harmony within, and that the seed of *unity consciousness* is present in every situation. When the primordial One is transformed into Two, some particles of One, with a minimal tendency to antagonise and a large affinity towards unity, stayed in the mutual territory of the new Creation *(vesica pisces)* as the strongest connection to the initial One. Through them, the divine parent makes sure she/he will always be remembered. On the other hand, opposite elements define the boundaries of Creation so it is advisable to recognise rather than negate them. That way we affirm a wider picture in which duality can be appreciated for what it is – an inherent quality of life, particularly explored at certain evolvement stage of consciousness.

While we are experiencing duality and learning from it, our yearning to go back to Unity gets stronger. Actually, we all have a memory of the primordial Unity and seek to return to it. By gradually removing conditioning of *dualistic consciousness* we endeavour to be *One with All That Is*. Even though our consciousness will change, expressions like light/dark, heavens/Earth, male/female, possible/impossible, pain/pleasure, will remain our linguistic reference to the dualistic nature of the Creation and its extremes that we witness. Human ability to balance, and therefore neutralise extremes, will bring peace to the world.

*Archangel Michael
through Ronna Herman*[II-2.5]

Each distorted, negative thought-form that you return to balance is one more obstacle that you remove from the collective mass consciousness of humanity.

▶ *2.2.7 – Not-Two
– painting by Milena*

*My invisible part of me,
Without you even this visible Me
Will lose her meaning.*

Milena

The invisible me is within the Universal Totality. It is the spiritual double (essence energy) that belongs to me. All my lives are the opportunities and efforts to purify myself and to evolve so that I can deserve and claim the spiritual wealth of my essence-self. The call of that self is here to lead me. After I transcend the ego and all fears, after I take my thoughts and my personality under full control, by gradually strengthening my *individual will* (to surpass the *partial will* that God gave me) – I will surrender to the *Will of the Total*, bringing all my belongings to the Total. When the *wills* merge[II-2.4], this visible terrestrial body will unite with the indestructible energies of its spiritual essence and produce an everlasting whole of the Real (everlasting) Me. The mighty energy of the universe will thereafter effortlessly flow through me, reinforcing me by all its might.

The fundamental goal of the *divine plan* is for us to complete this cycle hence manifest our full evolutionary potential.

EVERYONE IS CORRECT

The shift to *unity consciousness* will be accelerated through the heightening of our ability to control our own negative emotions, thoughts and actions, and through the use of the language that promotes this consciousness. We are to look for a win-win situation in any business, diplomacy, or a private dispute, and to be careful in qualifying the statements of others. Since everyone goes through programmes in his/her own energy dimension and, as there is no way we can know of the life plans involved, we cannot therefore judge and easily consider as untrue something that may look like that to us.

The truth is a matter of resonance. Since what resonates with one does not necessary resonate with another, everyone is right. No one is wrong – we just create and go through our own learning mediums. There are only necessary processes, all equally precious in this school of life, thus there are no good and bad experiences. Polarities like good/bad, truth/untruth, success/failure, right/wrong, need to be approached carefully and with awareness that between the poles they represent, in a great richness of manifestation, the value and choice of the golden middle path are always present. Therefore, by changing the way we see extreme qualities, our lifeboat will travel more smoothly without abruptly hitting the shores. Even if it touches one of the shores, we learn that we do not need to disembark but let go of that experience and continue flowing. Shores, as a metaphor of extremes, will become needless stations on our life-journey.

▲ *2.2.8 – As above, so below; as below so above – divine symmetry of Creation illustrated with the shape born from* **vesica pisces**

When you cling to a hairbreadth of distinction, heaven and earth are set apart.
If you want to realize the truth, don't be for or against.

Seng Ts'an

▲ *2.2.9 – The golden middle path is a choice of a consciousness that knows how to focus*

Through your loving
Existence and non-existence merge.
All opposites unite.
All that is profane Becomes sacred again.

Mevlana Celaleddin-i Rumi

WHAT WE BELIEVE, WE PROVE TO OURSELVES

Dyad exposes both the tension between opposing elements and their harmonious interaction. This paradox of tension and harmony is a core principal of Creation. The most obvious example is found in the dynamic relationship of the *man-woman* pair of opposites, whose longing for unity has secured the continuation of human life on this planet so far.

In the human mind, the heavens and Earth are traditionally seen as two separate and opposing realities. But, in actuality, we have never been separated by anything but by our own beliefs. The same factor of belief is crucial in the pair *possible/impossible*. That which we believe we prove to ourselves through our experience and consequently our experience serves as the best illustration of our beliefs.

The energy of our thoughts is stuck in our beliefs, and that very energy accumulation leads towards the manifestation of our beliefs. Even though beliefs hold our energy in the old and thus deprive it of the new, we see no reason to change them or live without them. So, to maintain certain comfort, we continue to believe what we believe and select proofs of our truths. Understanding this mechanism of cause and effect can liberate us from many rigid behavioural patterns that rob lots of our energy.

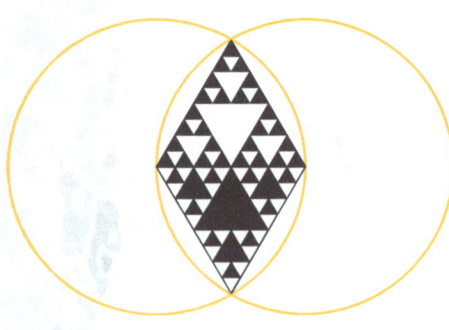

▲ 2.2.10 – *Opposites are divinely balanced*

Your world reflects every one of your thoughts, the good, the bad, and the ugly. You on some level are responsible for creating what you are living at this time. On a daily basis we have about 86,400 thoughts (waking & sleeping). About 60,000 of those thoughts are negative, self-defeating, and from the past. (What we once did, who once hurt us, what once happened.)

Every time you find yourself worrying, being negative, or thinking about injustices of the past, just say NO, say STOP! Cancel, Clear, Delete, get them the heck out of Dodge City!

Take control of your thoughts, your world, and your life. By being responsible for your thoughts you will begin to create a world that truly reflects your heart desires.

Gillian MacBeth-Louthan (Quantum Newsletter)

LIGHT AND DARK

The *light* and the *dark* are a dualistic set of the most generalised expression of opposite forces. They nicely illustrate that everything in existence has its opposite aspect which helps define it. Because there is only light, and One; every polarisation is also relative and illusory. Dark is a matter of perception, and perception is subject to choice. However, in the reality that we occupy, the working of dark and light is also experienced through interplay of *fear* and *love*.

Fear is a most fertile ground for manipulation and is a tool of the dark. It generates further experiences in the range of lower frequencies such as pain, hatred, greed, violence, destruction, war and manifests deficiencies. Despite its nature, we cannot say that fear is bad. It just does what it is meant to – by constriction, it opposes the expansion force of love/light contributing to an overall balance.

In the reality of the 3rd evolutionary dimension, the cycles of existence unfold through the stages between birth and death with the destruction-construction forces at work all the time. Both of these forces are ultimately creative. The difference between them is the same as the difference between fear and love: fear creates limitation and illusion of separation while love creates just the opposite – a sense of profound connectedness and unity. One force prompts dissension, the other ascension. Hence, fear ultimately leads to our destruction, since it closes the energy channels of our cells disabling their regeneration, while love is our first food and the key evolution catalyst.

UNITY CONSCIOUSNESS (A+B+C) :
Based on common elements (C) and an awareness of unity.
Recognises opposites (A – B) and, aiming at unity, works on their reconciliation.

For the last three thousand or so (years) human society has functioned in a predominantly masculine mode and is now quite out of balance. If you consider masculine energy to be represented by rationality, concern with the physical, forceful, expansive and individualistic; and the feminine by a tendency to be inclusive, intuitive, connecting and compassionate – then most will agree we need a swing of the pendulum towards the latter. The natural law about balance is that it must be weighted towards the feminine for creative growth to proceed. Otherwise growth (in terms of higher quality) is arrested, and degeneration takes place.

Alick Bartholomew
Hidden Nature

VESICA PISCES

symbol of duality
and its resolution

◀ 2.2.11 – *Illustration of dualistic and unity consciousness*

PROPERTIES EXHIBITED	PROPERTIES CREATED
Compassion	Love
Gratitude	Abundance
Tolerance	Harmony
Self-sacrifice	Beauty
Patience	Joy
Giving	Balance
Honour	Continuity
Kindness	Enlightenment
Understanding	Transformation
Cooperation	Empowerment
Care	Peace/Inner peace
Non judging	Fulfilment
Unconditional Love	Sense of Unity

Both light and shadow Are the dance of Love. Love has no cause; It is the astrolabe of God's secrets. Lover and Loving are inseparable and timeless.

Mevlana Celaleddin-i Rumi

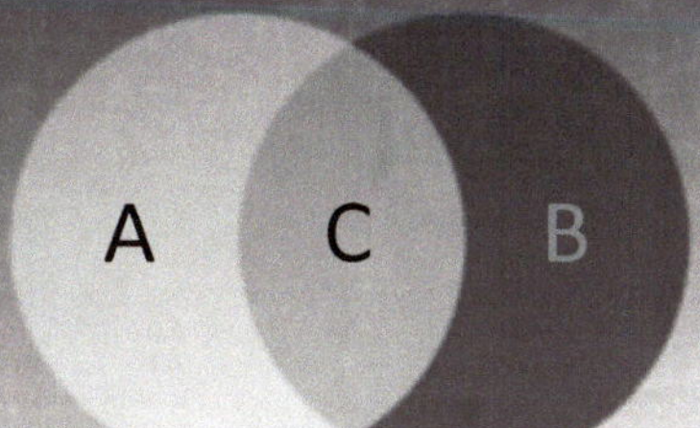

A – LIGHT

Love
Good
Truth
Winning
Right
Pleasure
Success
Modest
Pretty

B – DARK

Hatred/Fear
Bad
Lie
Losing
Wrong
Pain
Failure
Arrogant
Ugly

DUALISTIC CONSCIOUSNESS (A – B) :
Experiences Creation from the standpoint
of its extremes until it starts to recognise
the option of the middle ground (C)
and to appreciate its beauty and power.
Promotes conflict as well as a sense of separation.

VESICA PISCES PORTAL (C) :
Womb of Creation and the source of
unity consciousness
Passage between spiritual
and material

Love is a great Vibration which cannot be fitted into petty Feelings. If you notice We say Vibration, We do not say Feeling. Feelings are Your Physical Desires, they are not Love.

The Knowledge Book (F12, p 183, par 2)

CHOOSING LOVE

▲ 2.2.12 – *Evolvement steps of love*(II-2.6). *The achieved virtues are to be evident through our behaviours, rather than our thoughts*

The dualistic drama, culminating at the moment on our planet, clearly exposes its actors in accordance to the consciousness they choose to operate through. Yet, due to God's perfect playwriting and directing skills, the character one happens to play is surely ideally suited to one's evolutionary needs.

In this divine performance, what counts most is to participate. Since energies on the Earth continuously fluctuate, we need to adjust to them. Hence we also change by going through events that give us experiences necessary for the evolution of the energy and consciousness we epitomise. That is why, all we go through is equally important. It is therefore wise to accept everything surrendering to the Will of God. Genuine love and faith enable us to see His perfection only, in all aspects of life, and they are the base of unconditional acceptance. The love towards the Total is unshakable and conscious love. In it, our habit of judging things, people and events, subsequently becomes outdated manner of the *dualistic consciousness. Conscious love* sees dark as a tool used by light to purify and balance the Creation prompting higher states of being.

The programme of learning through opposites provides the fastest way of learning the truth. *No pain no gain* is just one example of this programme which is in effect on a certain level of evolution. But, as we start to understand duality and its purpose, we go more easily through our experiences. By merging the theses and antitheses, we find the truth in the precious middle. The middle path is the one which remembers oneness because it does not give priority to any extreme but to their reconciliation. So, it chooses to tame polarities in the name of unity and the whole. It chooses to operate through the forces of attraction, rather than repulsion that is also present in every *Dyad*.

Only evolved love can take the middle path. Love expressed through the *unity consciousness* brings harmony, peace and abundance.

Love is the vibration that supports life forms throughout Creation. It is the tool for activating our inherent divine power. Hence the evolvement dimensions we achieve are parallel to our ability to love.

In the World, Love flowing from the Essence is Pure, Natural Love. But Love put into action is an Evolutionary and Universal Love. And the factor taking into Effect and Supervising this Love attains Value parallel to the Evolutions and Consciousnesses of people.

The word Love Expressed through Speech is a frequency Total in "All Languages". If the Frequency of Love gets out of the thought and settles in one's Essence, that person never again utters the word Love. That person shows and exhibits his/her Love through his/her deed. This Situation is the "Saturation State of Love".

Vedia Bülent (Önsü) Çorak (Light)

Science shows... Love is the GLUE that Holds things Together – Daniel Winter(II-2.7)

FOUR

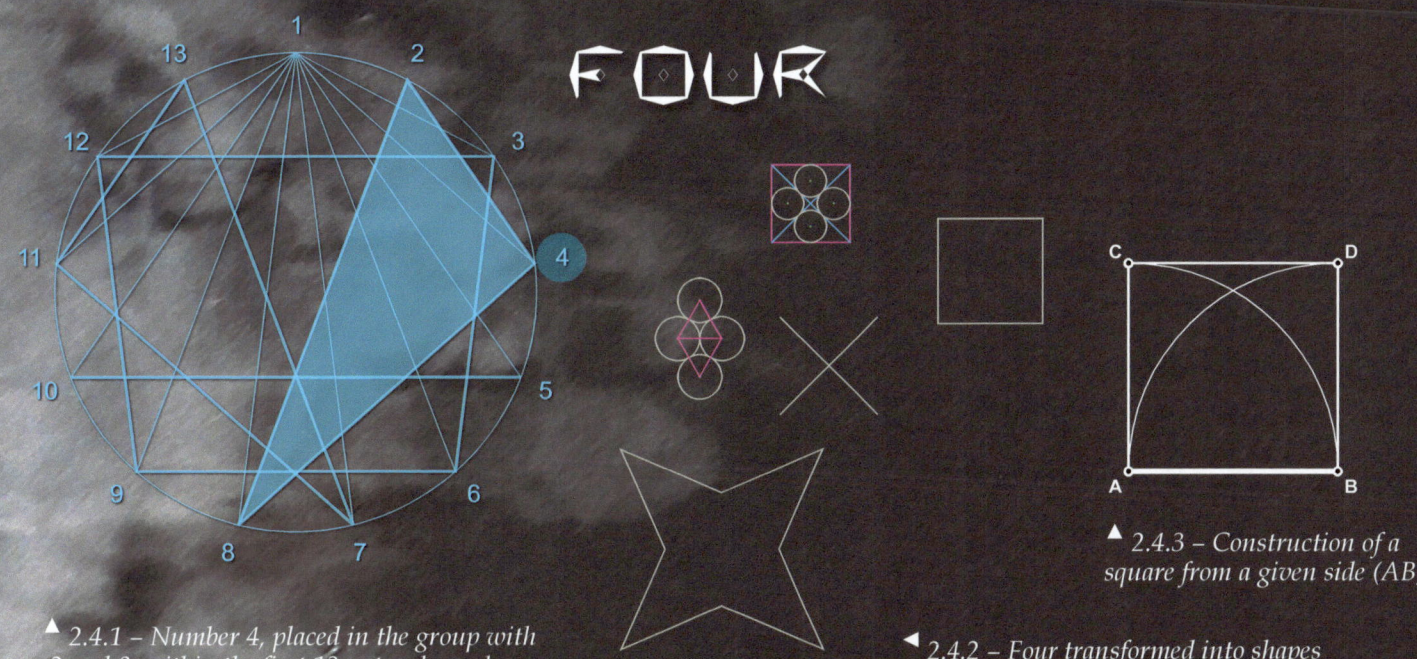

▲ 2.4.1 – Number 4, placed in the group with 2 and 8, within the first 13 natural numbers

◀ 2.4.2 – Four transformed into shapes

▲ 2.4.3 – Construction of a square from a given side (AB)

METAPHOR OF JUSTICE

After the manifestation of Three, as a triangle and a plane, the next creative step of the primordial source was marked with the appearance of Four, as a square.

For the Pythagoreans, the *Tetrad* (*Four*) was a symbol of completion, being the last one in the series 1, 2, 3, 4 to define the *tetraktys* (Fig. 1.1). Ten dots (1+2+3+4=10) arranged in a triangular formation were the key of Pythagorean philosophy and the *Tetrad* was the number of mathematical sciences they revered most of all: music, arithmetic, geometry and astronomy.

To the ancient Greeks, the *Tetrad* also represented fairness. The inspiration for this belief they found in the arithmetical characteristic of the number Four itself: 2+2=4, 2x2=4, as well as in the evenness and the perfect equality of its further components: (1+1)+(1+1)=4.

All I have said to you today is coming from God. He speaks:

*My children,
Protect the freedom of your soul!
Preserve the power of your spirit!
Sustain the light of your mind!
Maintain the goodness of your heart!*

In the human life, these four rules represent the music, art, wealth and strength.

Peter Deunov[II-4.1]

▲ 2.4.4 – Four circles give birth to a square

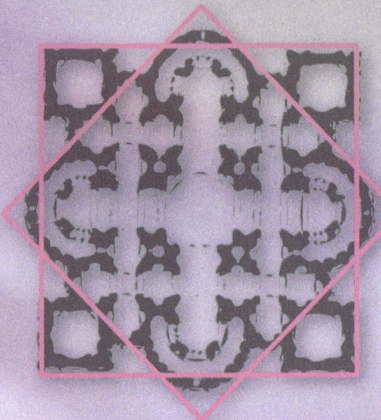

◀ 2.4.5 – *Number Four working through Eight – Bramante's design for the New St. Peter's Basilica in Rome, built 1506-1615*(II-4.2)

◀ 2.4.6 – *Symbol of the Directing Mechanism of the DIVINE PLAN*(II-8.8)

Each Cell carries the Secrets belonging to the past. It possesses the Power of the entire Universe. And it is a Universal Consciousness.

Mankind can make a single Cell, but can never make the Whole of it. Because, the intensified Energy in it is not an Energy known by the Mediums of the World.

It is divided into two, then to four, then to eight, then to sixteen and to thirty two. Then, it becomes a ball. It is fed by the water within it.

The Vibrations it emanates protect it from Negative Powers. Each Cell performs the Duty peculiar to it with success in the Medium suitable for its existence, according to the Command it receives from its Awareness of Consciousness.

The Knowledge Book
(F5, p 64, par 3-6)

FOURNESS

Many things are naturally arranged or seen by us through Fours. There are four phases of the Moon, four cardinal directions, four suits in a deck of cards, four wings on a bee, and sometimes four leaves on a clover – which makes us feel lucky when we find it.

In a DNA molecule, four nitrogen bases are used to make up the genetic code determining the distinctive form of every human, plant and animal. *Quad* also means *four*, as in the word *quadruped* where it indicates a four-footed animal.

It is generally accepted that the number Four and the square stand for four directions, four seasons and four cardinal winds. These meanings are derived from the Earth-Sun relationship in which two equinoxes and two solstices, as four cardinal points of a year, mark the turning points of the seasons. Fourness is associated with stability, groundedness, nurturing, and building for the future.

To the ancient Greeks, the *Tetrad* also represented four archetypal elements, each having a corresponding *Platonic solid*: earth – *cube,* air – *octahedron,* fire – *tetrahedron* and water – *icosahedron*. These elements were associated with the inner world of human virtues and the ancient symbols of the four states of matter: solid, gas, liquid and light. A tetrahedron, in particular, is associated with fourness since it is a type of a regular pyramid with four corners, and four faces made of equilateral triangles.

▲ 2.4.7 – *The number Four in a flower – cheerful and graceful*

SQUARING THE CIRCLE

The square is the most recognisable visual representation of a *Tetrad* and it is a symbol of the material world and earthly knowledge as opposed to the circle which speaks of the mystery of the embryonic One. The square inscribed into the circle therefore can be seen as the knowledge from the absolute source available to our evolutionary dimension (Fig. 2.4.9a).

Since the Creator has instilled in us a need to strive towards a better self, towards His perfection, we grow by continuously transcending our levels of knowledge and consciousness. Aspiring to reach God, symbolised by a circle, we aspire to realise our own infinite potential yet we also face numerous limitations posed both by our own selves and our life medium. How realistic that target is, can be illustrated by a geometrical puzzle called *squaring the circle* (Fig. 2.4.9b). To the philosophical mind this task of *squaring the circle* represents a mathematical model for challenging discovery of the ideal meeting/relationship between me and the Total, the mundane and the divine.

The relationship between the circle and the square has been a long-lasting subject of debate throughout the history of the *squaring the circle* theme. *Squaring the circle* means constructing a square of the same area as the given circle, with a compass and ruler only. The expression was also expanded to mean the identification of a square and circle where the perimeter of the square equalled the circumference of the circle.

◀ 2.4.8 – Harmonic diminution of the square

There is no higher truth than pure symmetry as it lives like a fractal rose in your heart.

Daniel Winter

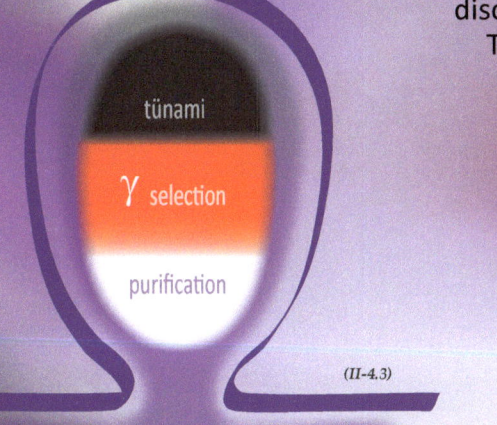

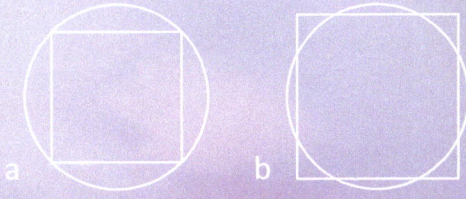

▲ 2.4.9 – Finding our place within the infinite – understanding matter in relation to the Spirit

◀ 2.4.10 – Ankh, an ancient Egyptian symbol of life and living, merges curved and straight lines that represent the world of Spirit and the world of matter. (OMEGA superimposed by Milena)

Matching the intangible (circle) with the tangible (square) in a meaningful and harmonious way, to the ancient minds also meant defining the point of transformation from Spirit to matter. The first recorded attempt in this direction dates back to 1650BC and Egypt. In the *Rhind Papyrus*, first translated and explained in 1877, **Ahmes**[II-4.4] (1680BC-1620BC) writes: *Cut off 1/9 of a diameter and construct a square upon the remainder; this has the same area as the circle* (Fig. 2.4.11). This construction of the square, using 8/9 of the circle's diameter, results in π being 3.16049 (or 256/81) which is 0.6% larger than the value of this *irrational number*.

▲ 2.4.11 – Ancient Egyptian attempt to square the circle (c1650BC)

The ancient Greeks also grappled with this mathematical puzzle. So many among them attempted to solve it and even earned the nickname *circle squarers*. **Archimedes**[II-4.5] (287BC-212BC) made an interesting discovery regarding the geometrical definition of the area of a circle. He related it to a triangle, thus showing how the area of a circle equals the area of a right-angled triangle – one of its sides equalling the radius and the other the circumference of the given circle (Fig. 2.4.12).

▲ 2.4.12 – **Archimedes'** way to geometrically present the area of a circle

Some historians tend to see the ancient Greeks as the people who used the *squaring the circle* riddle to teach philosophical principles based on geometry. At the entrance to **Plato's Academy**[II-4.6] in ancient Athens it reads: *Let none ignorant of Geometry enter here*. Such was their esteem for this mathematical discipline. However, today many believe that the Greeks did not realise that *squaring the circle* was impossible to solve because at that time π was not truly understood in its irrational and constant nature. More than 3000 years after **Ahmes** came close to the real value of π, **J. H. Lambert**[II-4.7] (1728-1777) explained and proved in 1761 that π was an *irrational number*.

▲ 2.4.13 – The cross, is a symbol of earthly and heavenly union. It also represents the two evolution phases of human consciousness – the horizontal (religious) and the vertical (universal), which we need to complete in order to reach our godly essence[II-4.8].

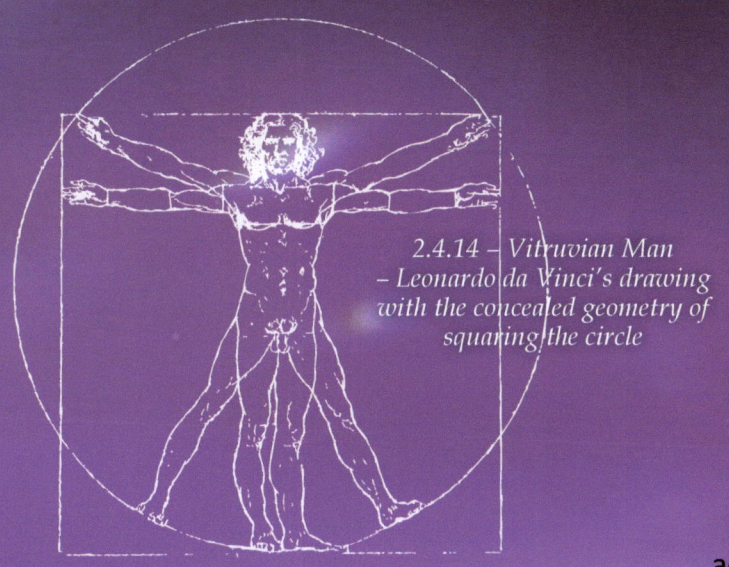

2.4.14 – *Vitruvian Man – Leonardo da Vinci's drawing with the concealed geometry of squaring the circle*

At some time a division within the *circle squarers* appeared creating two groups: those mathematically inclined, who also worked towards understanding the irrationality of π and defining it, and those led by an inexhaustible enthusiasm but without a serious mathematical approach. In 1775, because so many would claim to have found a solution for the *squaring the circle*, the French Academy of Science refused to examine new applications by passing a resolution that would regulate them. Despite numerous claims to a solution, many also tried to prove it impossible to solve and would consider it the highest mathematical achievement of all times.

Since the circle is a figure related to the *irrational number* π, its area can never be precisely calculated. It is only infinitesimally approximated for it is a function of π and its evasive nature. On the other hand, the area of the square is precisely definable within the domain of rational numbers so it is a great challenge to equalise the area values of these two geometrical forms.

The symbolic aspect of this great puzzle illustrates the way the Spirit (circle) has created a comprehensible world of matter (square), or how the heavens and Earth can harmoniously coexist. It is a mathematical metaphor of the transformation of infinity to its finite form.

In his book *The ANCIENT SECRET of the FLOWER OF LIFE*, **Drunvalo Melchizedek**[II-4.10] talks about levels of consciousness in terms of the geometry of *squaring the circle*. According to **Melchizedek**, the level of consciousness of any human being in Creation can be determined by analysing the relationship between the square and the circle that fits around his/her body.

The squaring of the circle... could even be called the archetype of wholeness.

Carl Gustav Jung[II-4.9]

▲ 2.4.15 – *Squaring the circle*

◀ 2.4.16 – *Life is the interplay of opposite forces. When harmonised, they express an order and beauty.*

EIGHT

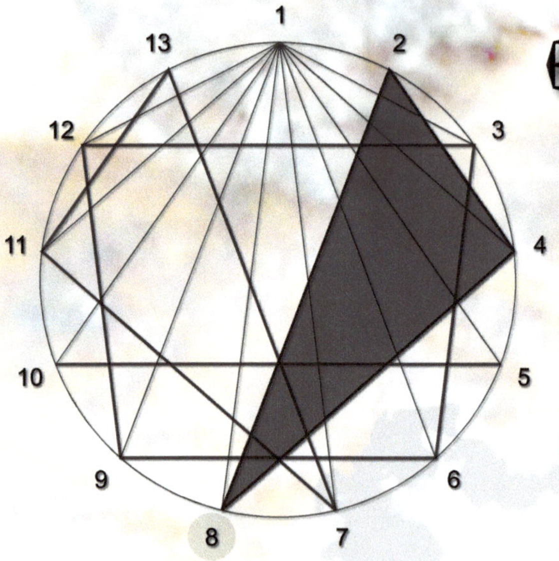

> *Universe is composed of a symphony of alternating currents with the harmonies played on a vast range of octaves.*
>
> Nikola Tesla[II-8.1]

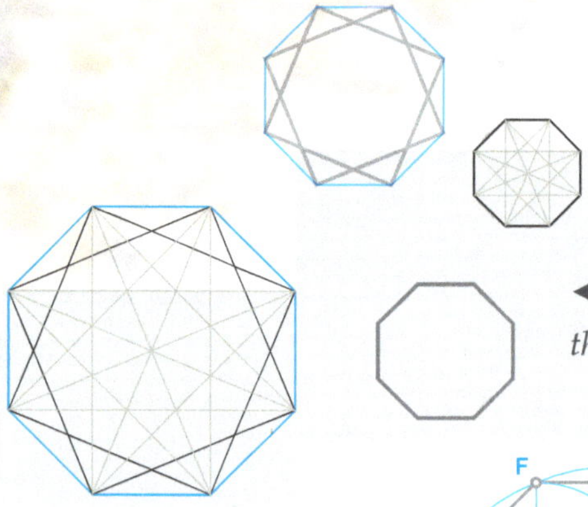

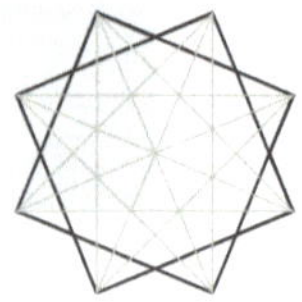

◀ 2.8.2 – Patterns born from the number Eight

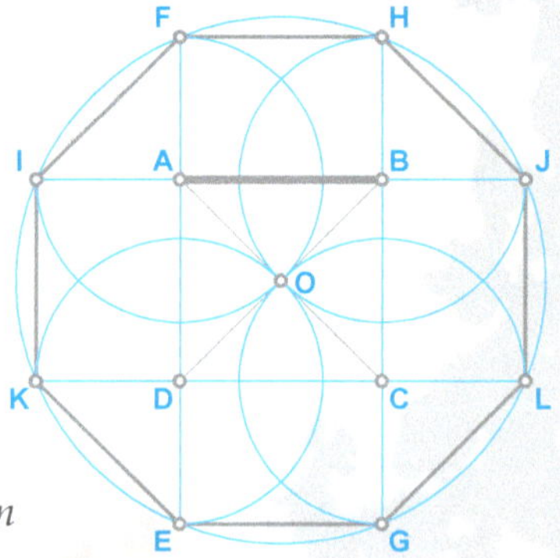

▲ 2.8.1 – Number 8, placed in the group with 2 and 4, within the first 13 natural numbers

▶ 2.8.3 – Construction of a regular octagon

SELF-RESONANCE

Part of the nature of the number Eight is determined by its dividers One, Two and Four, and its closeness to the number Seven.

Eight, or the *Octad* in Greek, signifies rhythmical repetition that exhibits no sameness but rather a state of self-resonance. That quality is captured in music in the case of an *octave* which is the interval between the given note and its new expression sounding eight notes higher or lower. In terms of frequency, the ratio between the beginning note and the one at the *octave* distance is 1:2 or 2:1. This halving/doubling of frequencies on the way to higher self-expression is an element of the *Dyad* working within the *Octad*.

The appearance of an *octave* is the result of seven notes (steps) proceeding until the point of qualitative change in the eighth step is reached. In the language of arithmetic, an *octave* is: 7n+1. The eighth step is one of renewal in which the initial qualities resonate through their new value acquired from the experience of the seven-step-journey. On every Monday we symbolically enter a new personal *octave* on the journey called *life on Earth*.

The number Eight can also be seen as a vertically placed symbol of infinity (Fig. 2.8.4).

◀ 2.8.4 – The concept of infinity, denoted by the lemniscate symbol, is preserved in the number Eight. The Knowledge Book clarifies that this symbol is derived graphically by connecting two Greek letters (Alpha), and represents a segment of the spiral vibrations as well as their operational style[II-8.2].

RESONANCE – THE WAY OF HARMONY

Our relation to the world, and to people, is governed by the principle of resonance. Since everything is energy vibrating at its particular frequency, only frequency bands that we can harmonise with can make sense within the energy field of our being.

Comfort in our perception is the sign of personal truth. What resonates with us is what appeals to us and what we can consider to be the truth. We can find ourselves feeling uncomfortable, irritated, spaced-out or generally upset within some frequencies. Thus, our personal truths and affinities are a matter of frequency compatibility between us and a given subject.

Understanding God differs from person to person. Thus we can say that there are as many versions of Gods as there are individuals contemplating God.
Since individual perceptions and experiences depend on the consciousness level of a person, our understanding of God also changes in line with our evolvement.
Our changing frequencies gradually get into resonance with the divine waves.

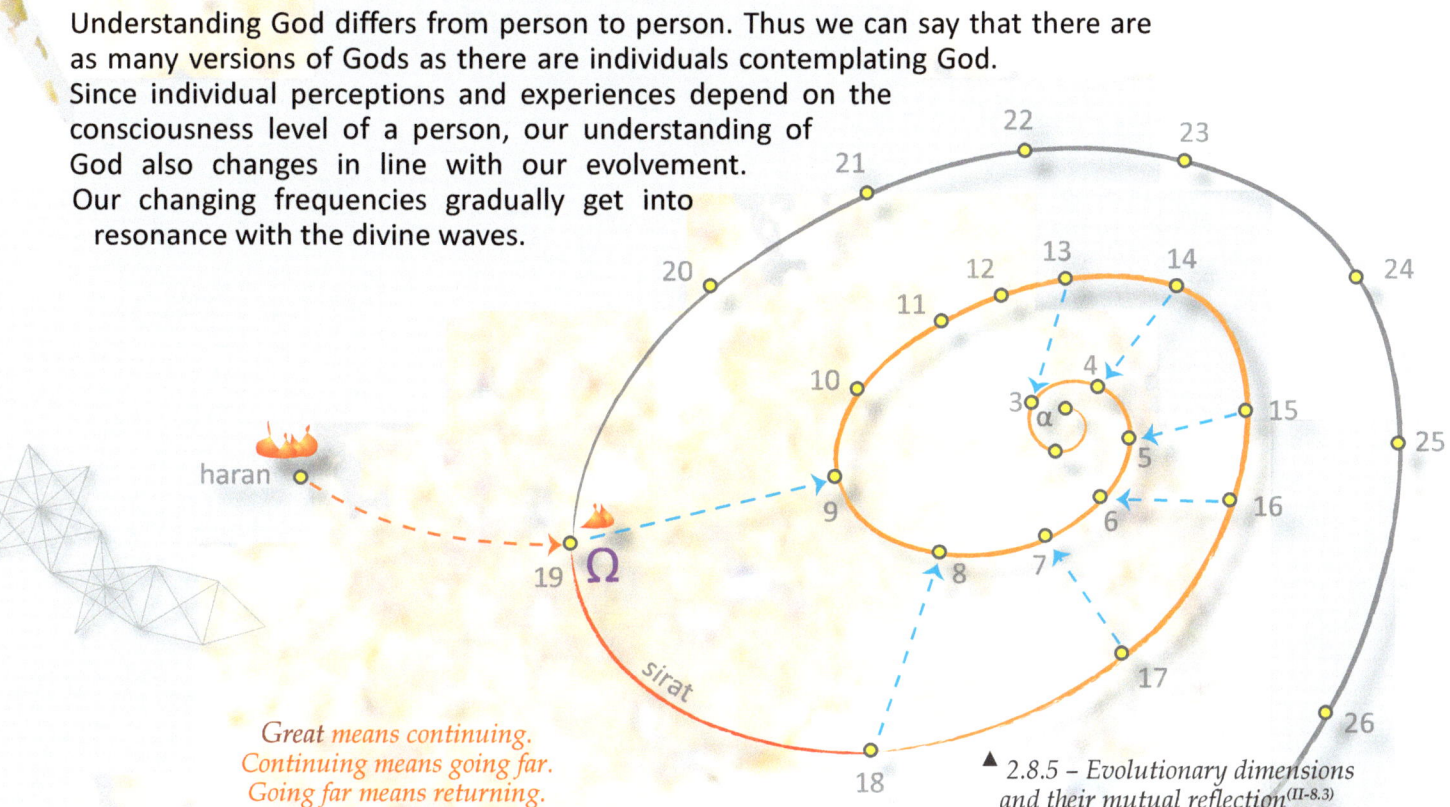

▲ 2.8.5 – Evolutionary dimensions and their mutual reflection[(II-8.3)]

Great means continuing.
Continuing means going far.
Going far means returning.

Lao Tzu
(Tao Te Ching)

Our relationships with people are also influenced by the frequencies we epitomise. Energy emissions from other people which can harmoniously continue to vibrate in our personal energy field, by properly nesting in it, have a future in our biology. On the other hand, those emissions which cannot construct a sustainable relationship with our energies are destined not to last through us. Any *modus operandi* that is not life supporting is doomed to fail.

Resonance is nature's way of enabling harmony to guide processes and to continuously advance existing states. Our role is to consciously direct our being towards its highest expression. While endeavouring to do this, our most powerful tool is the ability to change ourselves and, as a consequence, incur change on the outside. That is the only way we can fairly influence life. When we place ourselves in the frequencies of love, peace and harmony, we emit the frequencies of those states and through the law of resonance influence the environment. So, by purifying ourselves we work for the betterment of all.

In the ordinance of the universes, each solar system is considered a whole characterised by specific evolutionary, energy and solar dimensions – for example: the 10th solar system corresponds to the 13th evolutionary dimension, the 52nd energy dimension, and the 11th solar dimension.
Energies of the higher solar dimensions are projected onto the lower solar dimensions. Hence, the energy of the 15th solar system, the dimension where The Quran was prepared, (the 18th evolutionary dimension = the 72nd energy dimension = the 16th solar dimension) is projected onto the 5th solar system (the 8th evolutionary dimension = the 32nd energy dimension = the 6th solar dimension).
Human evolution on our planet starts from the 3rd evolutionary dimension (the 12th energy dimension = the 1st solar dimension) therefore the energies of the 13th evolutionary dimension are regularly projected on it. However, in accordance with the programme of accelerated evolution, from the beginning of the 20th century, our planet is exposed to the showers of the cosmic energies coming from the 19th evolutionary dimension – called OMEGA (the 76th energy dimension = the 17th solar dimension = the 16th solar system). The Knowledge Book, reflects this energy to its own readers parallel to their consciousness level – owing to the cosmic technique called light-photon-cyclone present in the book.

RHYTHM OF CHANGE GOVERNED BY EIGHT

In the 92 elements of naturally occurring atoms, shown in the Periodic table of the elements[II-8.4], the rhythm of change evolves through the number Eight (Fig. 2.8.6). The reason the number Eight has become the pace and the order establisher, lies in the fact that the outermost electron shell of an atom can have a maximum of eight electrons.

Vertical columns in the Periodic table called *groups*, or *families*, are made of elements with the same number of electrons (between one and eight) orbiting in the outer shell of their atoms and that number is used to name the relevant *group*. Horizontal rows of elements crossing each *group*, viewed from the left to the right, add one more electron to the outer shell of the element in each *group*. The aim of this distribution is to fill the outer shell with up to eight electrons. The adding of matter happens gradually to atoms and its result creates the differences between the properties of the elements belonging to neighbouring *groups*. The recurring regularity of the number of electrons in the outer shell is responsible for the similarity in the properties of elements within each *group* or, in other words, the resonance of the common properties throughout the *group*. Each horizontal row is an *octave* apart from the previous row.

The affinity of atoms to combine is also related to the number Eight, since each atom tends to have eight electrons in its valence shells — which gives it the same electronic configuration as that of a *noble gas* (*octet rule*).

$$1 \times 8 + 1 = 9$$
$$12 \times 8 + 2 = 98$$
$$123 \times 8 + 3 = 987$$
$$1234 \times 8 + 4 = 9876$$
$$12345 \times 8 + 5 = 98765$$
$$123456 \times 8 + 6 = 987654$$
$$1234567 \times 8 + 7 = 9876543$$
$$12345678 \times 8 + 8 = 98765432$$
$$123456789 \times 8 + 9 = 987654321$$

▲ *2.8.7 – Regularity generated through multiplication by Eight*

▼▲ *2.8.6 – Fragment of the Mendeleev Periodic Table*

The Periodic Table of the chemical elements has been arranged in various ways so far, including as octaves by John Newlands ("Law of Octaves" 1865). Chemical elements were also positioned along one or more spirals or circles which would spatially evolve into cones, cylinders or even spheres. Crookes (1898), for example, arranged elements along the spiral evolving into two cylinders. The base of these joint cylinders was in the form of the number Eight.

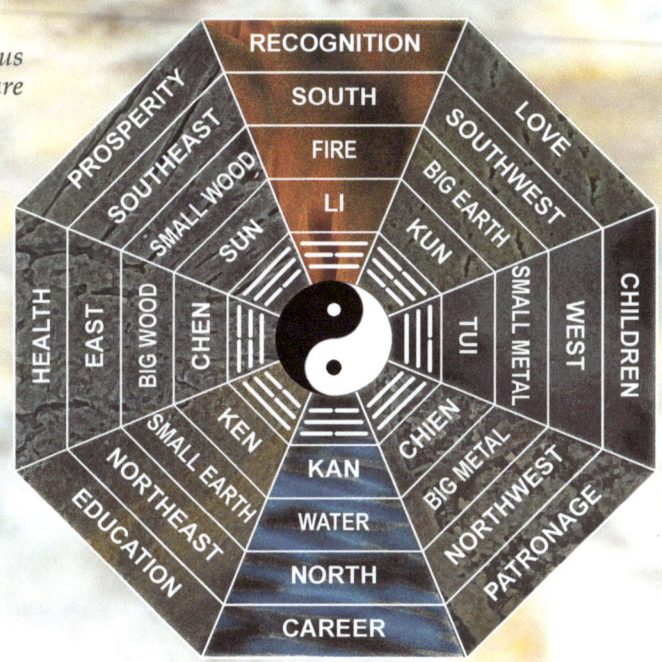

▶ 2.8.8 – *Pa Kua is an energy map that helps us understand our relation to nature*

*Change has an absolute limit:
This produces two modes;
the two modes produce four forms,
the four forms produce eight trigrams;
the eight trigrams determine fortune
and misfortune.*

Confucius

The number Eight plays a significant role in an ancient Chinese divination tool called *I Ching* (also known as *The Book of Change*). More than 4000 years ago, the Chinese sage **Fu Hsi** defined *trigrams* which are fundamental to the philosophy of *I Ching*. Each trigram is the story of life forces recorded in a combination of broken (*Yin*) and solid (*Yang*) lines taken three at a time. There are eight such possible combinations of *Yin* and *Yang*, hence there are eight basic trigrams, or eight stages of transformation caused by the constant play of opposites. Later on, these were arranged into 64 *hexagrams* (six-line figures) to complete this peculiar cosmological model.

As a divination instrument, *I Ching* is used to explain all phenomena of life. Earthly and celestial matters are understood and linked through the force of *Tao* (or *Dao*) and they are alone considered an expression of its eternal flow and change. However, certain regularities within the change are observed and depicted in *trigrams* and *hexagrams*: the 64 *hexagrams* positioned in a circle, or a square, represent the continuous process of creation spontaneously manifested through the interaction between *Yin* and *Yang*.

The eight basic trigrams, when used in Chinese *fengshui*[II-8.5] tradition, are placed onto an octagonal symbol called *Pa Kua* (Fig. 2.8.8). *Pa Kua* relates and combines eight starting trigrams of *I Ching*, that occupy eight directions, with five elements, seasons and some aspects of human life.

As well as in the *I Ching*, the number Eight is also the key used in the ancient game of *chess*. According to Sumerian cosmogony that **Ahura Mazda** (*One Uncreated Creator of All*) gave through **Zarathustra**, a chess board mirrors the universe made of *time*, *force* (energy), *space* and *matter* (Fig. 2.8.9). Two sets of sixteen forces act on its 64 squares. The white forces are the army of the Light of **Ahura Mazda** and are made up of the positive forces of Nature (*Fravashis*) and the Cosmos (*Arhuras*). The black forces are the army of their shadow: the negative forces of Nature (*Khrafstras*) and the Cosmos (*Devas*), reigned over by **Ahriman**. Man is one of the *Fravashis* and the most important partner of the Creator. His role is to further the process of Creation within continuous battles of opposing forces that rule in the microcosm in which he lives. Thus, Man needs to learn to coexist with all forces by adjusting his own thoughts, words and deeds to them. Harmonising in this way enables Man to use existing forces as a source of energy and knowledge.

The ancient sages have managed to translate the highest principles of the natural forces and eternal cosmic laws into the rules of the game on the chess board, and through the combination of hexagrams of *I Ching*. The number Eight served to illustrate their understanding of the unchanging laws of the macrocosm.

EIGHT OF ODU IFA

Ifa is an ancient spiritual tradition of the Yoruba[II-8.6] people of West Africa. Knowledge and wisdom contained in their culture come from the cradle of civilisation in the Abyssinian highlands on the river Nile. From there, some scientists indicate, all earthly language originated and first migrated to Asia. The stream that has led to Asia is believed to be responsible for taking the *Ifa* as far as China, about 5,300 years ago, which helps us understand why the Chinese divination tool *I Ching* bears a resemblance to *Ifa* divination. However complex *I Ching* is, as a younger relative of *Ifa*, it seems to be Ifa's shorter version. *I Ching* uses 64 hexagrams made from the eight basic trigrams, while *Ifa* functions within the system of 256 configurations called *Odu*, mostly using sixteen of these.

Not only did *Ifa* spread to China, but to areas of North Africa, Spain in the early 12th century, Madagascar, and to the Americas with the African people where it is practised in its original way, but also altered and merged with the native traditions creating new ones such as *Vodou* (meaning *sacred*) in the West Indies. There are indications that *Tarot* also relates to *Ifa*.

Ifa divination is a ritual conducted by a *Babalawo* (Father of Secrets), a trained priest. He uses sixteen palm nuts and throws them in a particular way to obtain information for eight marks, to be placed in two columns, as a combination upon which a reading can be done. These combinations, as signs made of eight marks, are known as *Odu* and are seen as guidelines for realising personal destiny which *Ifa* followers believe, in general terms, has been chosen prior to coming to this world.

2.8.9 – In his book Zend Avesta, using point and line, Zarathustra explains the creation of the Universe

CREATOR — SUN
PRESERVER — WATER
ETERNAL LIFE — AIR
WISDOM — EARTH
WORK — FOOD
LOVE — HEALTH
PEACE — MAN
POWER — JOY

2.8.10 – The sixteen forces of nature and the cosmos, according to the teaching of Ahura Mazda

Each *Odu* has a name and wisdom which has been preserved as oral literature. During an *Ifa* session, the *Odu* obtained is chanted to advise the supplicant with a fresh, yet ancestral, context of thinking.

There are sixteen principal *Odu* patterns as there are sixteen eyes of the God **Fa**, or **Ifa**, who brought this system of learning to the people. Each principal *Odu* has sixteen subordinate ones making a total of 256 *Odu* patterns (16x16). Since every *Odu* is a combination of eight marks, and if we represent each one as a figure of an octagon, then the whole *Odu Ifa* can be shown as a matrix of 256 octagons.

	NAME	1	2	3	4
1	Ogbe	0	0	0	0
2	Oyeku	00	00	00	00
3	Iwori	00	0	0	00
4	Odi	0	00	00	0
5	Irosun	0	0	00	00
6	Iwonrin	00	00	0	0
7	Obara	0	00	0	00
8	Okanran	00	0	00	0
9	Ogunda	0	0	0	00
10	Osa	00	0	0	0
11	Ika	00	0	0	00
12	Oturupon	00	0	00	0
13	Otura	0	0	0	0
14	Irete	0	0	00	0
15	Ose	0	00	0	0
16	Ofun	00	0	00	0

2.8.11 – Sixteen major Odu of Ifa and their binary numbers

▼ 2.8.12 – Ika Meji, the 11th holy **Odu** of Ifa – painting by Funmi Odusolu(II-8.7)

If painting is an arrangement in colours, The Yoruba world is an arrangement in vibrations.
For us the universe is material and spiritual rhythm; And the process of arrangement of this rhythm is ritual, The gestalt of restitution, and the justification of God's ways.

Funmi Odusolu
(Yoruba artist, Nigeria)

EIGHTFOLD GEOMETRY

There are many examples offered by nature regarding the use of Eight in its creative action. An octopus is one of them. It exposes octagonal symmetry by spreading its eight tentacles. The spider, an insect-like creature with eight legs, is another example from the animal kingdom. It skilfully knits tiny webs of astonishing strength and beautiful linear geometry. Because of this ability, in some ancient cultures the spider was depicted as a symbol of a cosmic weaver and a mundane replica of the One who weaves the web of *All That Is*.

With the exception of the trivial example of the number One, the number Eight is the first cube (2x2x2=8) among the first ten numbers. One geometrical illustration of Eight is made of two squares one on top of the other where one is rotated 45 degrees. The resulting figure is called a (8/2) star-octagon or octagram (Fig. 2.4.6). In Hinduism it symbolises the eight kinds of wealth of the goddess **Lakshmi** and is known as the *star of Lakshmi*. The regular octagon was extensively applied in the architecture of Byzantine, Arab and Romanesque schools in the design of domes, towers and churches (Fig. 2.4.5).

▼ 2.8.13 – *Squares echoing through the number 256*

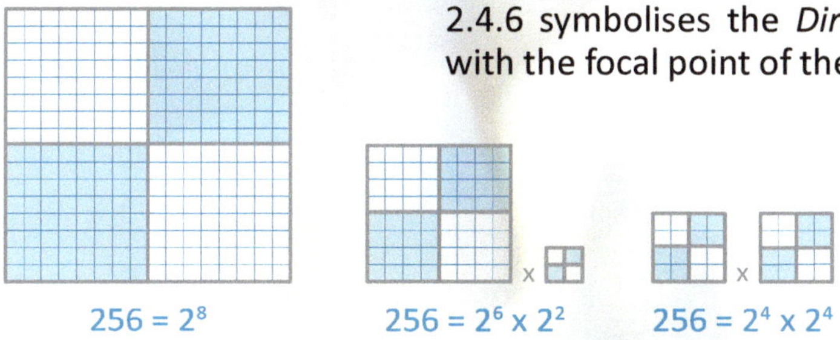

According to *The Knowledge Book*(II-8.8), the octagram featured in the illustration 2.4.6 symbolises the *Directing Mechanism of the divine plan*. By cooperating with the focal point of the *divine plan* (Fig. 2.6.10), this mechanism has projected to our planet the knowledge of the *seven terrestrial layers* and the *seven celestial layers* comprised in the sacred books. The next level of our evolution would require receiving and assimilation of the knowledge of the *seven universal layers,* which the Lord has sent to us with *The Knowledge Book*.

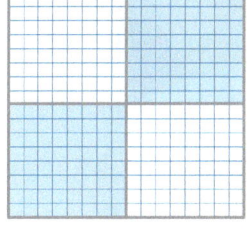

$256 = 2^8$

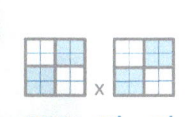

$256 = 2^6 \times 2^2$ $256 = 2^4 \times 2^4$

OCTAVES OF THOUGHTS

The phenomenon of the *octave*, related to the number Eight, is also significant for our inner world. In *The Ascended Master Instruction Book*(II-8.9), **St. Germain** talks about the *octaves of thought*. He recognises the following *octaves*:

8 – *octave of perfect happiness,*
7 – *octave of pure love* in which we feel the *mighty I AM presence,*
6 – *octave of joy* based on a recognition of God's power within us,
5 – *octave of tolerance* as a will to give to others freedom in thought and speech,
4 – *octave of criticism and condemnation* in which most of humanity operates,
3 – *octave of anger,*
2 – *octave of hate*
1 – *octave of crime.*

The first six *octaves*, which are below the *octave of pure love,* are primarily created by humans alienated from their own godly essence. God has never attempted to detach Himself from His Creation. On the other hand, Man consistently ignores his own godly potential demonstrating his alienation from God. From the *octave of tolerance* (5) we begin to access the light more significantly, and from the *octave of pure love* (7) we access the godly presence.

When we dwell in the lower *octaves of thoughts* not only do we function through the corresponding lower energies but we expose ourselves to the burden of a huge outpouring of the past and present accumulation of the collective energy of that particular *octave*. It is, therefore, very important to enter the higher *octaves of thoughts* by monitoring our thoughts, feelings and words.

In every moment, each person carries his/her own heaven or hell, depending on which *octave* it chooses to function from. There is no other cause of our mental and emotional states than our attitudes that have created them – clarifies **St. Germain**.

The Dimensions you are going to enter will be Powerful in proportion with the Power of the Potential of Your Love. Your Perceptions depend on the Powers of Your Frequencies. The Supervision here is for making You know Yourselves, find Yourselves. Only afterwards may You flutter Your wings in the infinity of Universal Dimensions.

The Knowledge Book
(F8, p 114, par 5)

◄ 2.8.14 – *This expression of Eight, gardeners call the Dahlia*

3 6 9 12

THREE

▲ 2.3.1 – Number 3, placed in the group with 6, 9 and 12, within the first 13 natural numbers

▲ 2.3.2 – Geometrical expressions of the number Three

◀ 2.3.3 – Construction of an equilateral triangle

▼ 2.3.4 – Every triangle is a geometrical echo of the Holy Trinity (a).

On the second day of Creation, a square and pentagon were also defined. Hence, the three figures that make the sides of the Platonic solids, emerged at the same time (b).

A NEW STEP, A NEW LEVEL OF EXPERIENCE

Every new step of Creation brings an authentic level of experience. With the manifestation of the third sphere, it was the plane defined by the triangle which was the very first shape delivered through the opening of the *vesica pisces*.

The ancient Greeks considered the number Three to be the first number with One and Two being the parent numbers. They called it the *Triad*, while some Native Americans used the expression *centre of the One*.

The *Triad* marks the birth of a triangle, which is a cardinal geometrical figure of the Creation and a metaphor for the sacred enclosure.

Triangular surfaces exhibit an exceptional stability. This quality originates from the ability of a triangle to balance opposing tendencies of internal forces, so that it would not require any outside support. The triangle is a superior building block for any structure.

▶ 2.3.5 – **Project of EXISTENCE** originates from the ATLANTA advanced civilisation, called Golden Dimension. In the *Tranquillity of Silences*, they firstly initiated an *energy formation* process and then the formation of the natural Gürz crystal, by following the Law of 18 Systems and its Mutation Programme. The existential programme unfolds according to the principle of reflection, One to Three and Three to One, being in effect in connection to Automatism[II-3.1].

> **Everything** has a beginning. However, this beginning has never become effective *Singly*. In accordance with the Programme of Existence, everything becomes effective by the *Reflection* of (THREE TO ONE – ONE TO THREE).
>
> *The Knowledge Book*
> *(S1, p 996, par 5)*

> *Three is the mystery, comes from the great one.*
>
> Thoth (*The Emerald Tablets*)

THREE AS ONE

In Christian tradition there is a *Holy Trinity* of the *Holy Father*, the *Son* and the *Holy Spirit*. Revered as a principal code of Creation, it is illustrated in numerous architectural and craft works through tripartite windows and partitions, in paintings and carvings as triptychs, and it is also found in the figure known as the *Borromean rings* (Fig. 2.3.7).

Borromean rings are a spatial figure made of three rings linked in such a way that no ring touches another, yet together they make a whole. Each ring acts as a binding factor for the remaining two, thus removing any one ring disconnects the others. It is this very bond which gives a special quality to the triune group. *Borromean rings* symbolise the synergy principle and its unique strength resulting from the high level of collaboration and loyalty within the group.

> *All of us are kin. All of us are siblings of the wondrous workings of the triune Godhead. We spring from the divine plan and, in each lifetime, have done our part to reveal the magic enclosed within the divine plan.*
>
> *Galactic Federation of Light through Sheldan Nidle*[II-3.2]

▶ 2.3.6 – Three returning to One

◀ 2.3.7 – **The Holy Trinity** of mind (thought), body (emotion) and Spirit (Soul), or Father-Mother-Child, or neutron-proton-electron, or a Triune Godhead – all depicted through the *Borromean link* of various geometric figures

I have just three things to teach: simplicity, patience, compassion. These three are your greatest treasures. – Lao Tzu

In India, **Brahma** – God of Creation, **Vishnu** – God of Preservation and **Shiva** – God of Dissolution, represent the Hindu Trinity of Gods of the continuous cosmic process. In *tantric* tradition the downward-pointing triangle is a symbol of **Shakti** – the creative feminine power or dynamic aspect of consciousness, while the upward-pointing triangle symbolises the male principle, or consciousness in its static state, and is the emblem of **Shiva**.

According to another school of Indian philosophy *(Samkhya)*, these two triangles stand for **Purusha** (Pure Consciousness) and **Prakriti** (Material World). The overlapping of the upward and downward-pointing triangles generally represents transcendence of duality through the dynamic merging of opposites, like male and female, Spirit and matter, static and kinetic (Fig. 2.6.10).

The glyph depicted in figure 2.3.8 is called a *triquetra*. It consists of three interlocked circle segments, as if taken from the central part of the *Borromean rings*. The *triquetra* also perfectly illustrates the unity aspect of *three as one*. As with *the Borromean rings*, it is used in many religious traditions to represent the *Holy Trinity*.

Two people can easily create a consensual reality by establishing their own agreed-upon truths. If a third person joins, the truth will be a result of all three of them meeting at the same coordinate. That is how Three return to One. Unity of this kind is strong and stable for it carries the properties of the number Three. The principle *three as one*, as a supreme trinity on the mundane level, was employed in ancient Rome, for a time, whilst the *triumvirate* was the governing body of that great empire.

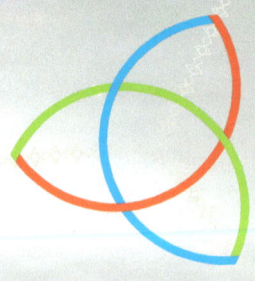

◀ *2.3.8 – The triquetra is a trefoil knot and a symbol of tripartite unity. This unity resembles an intangible embrace, yet a strong association and commitment. Peculiarly, a stable whole is achieved without the three interlocking elements physically touching one another. It seems as if this particular spatial relation is regulated on a higher dimensional level.*

TRIAD ENDS DUALITY

Three is inherent in the number Two because where there are two, there is a relationship between the two which further defines them. This relationship, as a third element can also be a mediator, neutral factor, or sometimes a witness, as well as the key to re-establishing the unity of the polarised *two*. The relationship has a power to bind the polarities into a stable whole. The *Triad* ends duality.

In fairy tales, the number *three* often appears in the form of challenges that symbolise three steps to an inner completion. There would usually be three wishes to be fulfilled, or tasks posed. Eventually, three-step efforts reconcile opposing forces with all settling in the comfort of an invigorated unity. Happiness is found in maturity, inner peace and enlightenment.

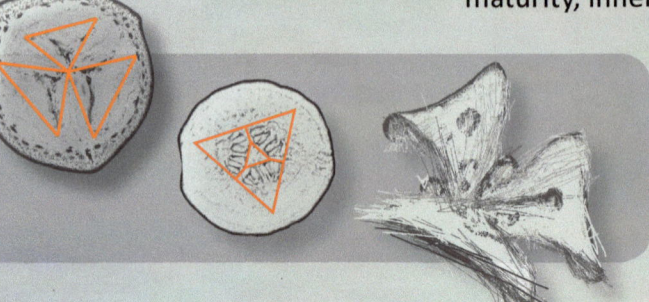

◀ *2.3.9 – Three-petal flower (Cat's Ear) – one of nature's way of talking about trinity*

◀ *2.3.10 – Cucumber and melon cuts, expose the symmetry of their inner structure based on the number Three*

ALL IS DIVIDED INTO THREE

The *Triad* is inherent in numerous life processes, and in the geometry of many forms, where it stands for a specific completeness. **Plato** believed that a surface was composed of triangles while **Homer** thought that All was divided into three.

In nature, we can observe structures based on number Three. Such structures are trees, which have the root, the trunk and the crown, as well as some fruits and vegetables like bananas, melons and cucumbers (Fig. 2.3.10).

Many colour modes have three primary colours. The figure 2.3.12 shows some of the most well known ones, used: A – in the mixing light (*red*, *blue* and *green*), B – on an artist's palette (*red*, *blue* and *yellow*) and C – in the medium of printing ink (*cyan, magenta* and *yellow*).

Esoteric teachings refer to three cosmic zones: the sky, the earth and the underworld. The active part of the day comprises morning, afternoon and evening. Human life has three major stages: childhood, adulthood and old age.

Within one cycle, there are a beginning, middle and an end.

NUMBER THREE IN SPACE

The Knowledge Book reveals the structure of a whole called *System* or *Unified Reality*, within the *Gürz crystal,* based on the number Three[II-3.3]:

3 GALAXIES = 1 Whole
6 Galaxies = 1 NOVA

3 Novas = 18 Galaxies = 1 COSMA = 1 Small UNIVERSE-NUCLEUS
3 Universe-Nuclei = 54 Galaxies = 1 GALAXY CLUSTER
9 Galaxy Clusters = 486 Galaxies
  = 27 Cosmas = 1 UNIVERSAL COLONY
18 Universal Colonies = 8748 Galaxies
  = 486 Cosmas = 1 COSMA UNIFICATION CENTRE.

Since 1 Cosma Unification Centre supervises 1 REALM:

8748 Galaxies = 1 REALM
18000 Realms = 1 COSMOS
1 Cosmos = 157464000 Galaxies

18 Cosmoses = 1 UNIVERSE
18000 Cosmoses = UNIVERSE OF THE SYSTEM
  = 1000 Universes = SYSTEM = UNIFIED REALITY.

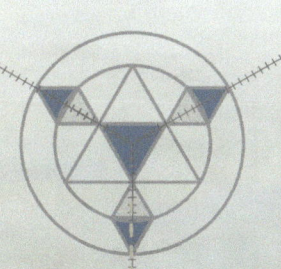

▼ 2.3.11 – Cosmic wheel

▼ 2.3.12 – Primary colours pertaining to:
A – Light,
B – The artist's palette and
C – Printing ink

Within a *Gürz crystal* there are 1800 *mini atomic wholes.* Each one of them represents one *existential dimension* and has its own *System –* which it is obliged to serve.

All 1800 *Systems* form the *Gürz System* and serve the *All-Merciful,* the director of the *Gürz System.*

The fractal organisation of this celestial unity of high order is visible in the geometry of the *Gürz crystal.*

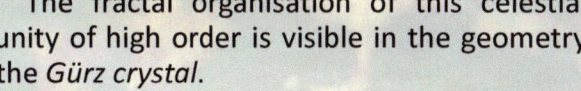

Monad moves towards Diad and stops at Triad. – St. Gregory of Nazianzus (Theologus)

Six

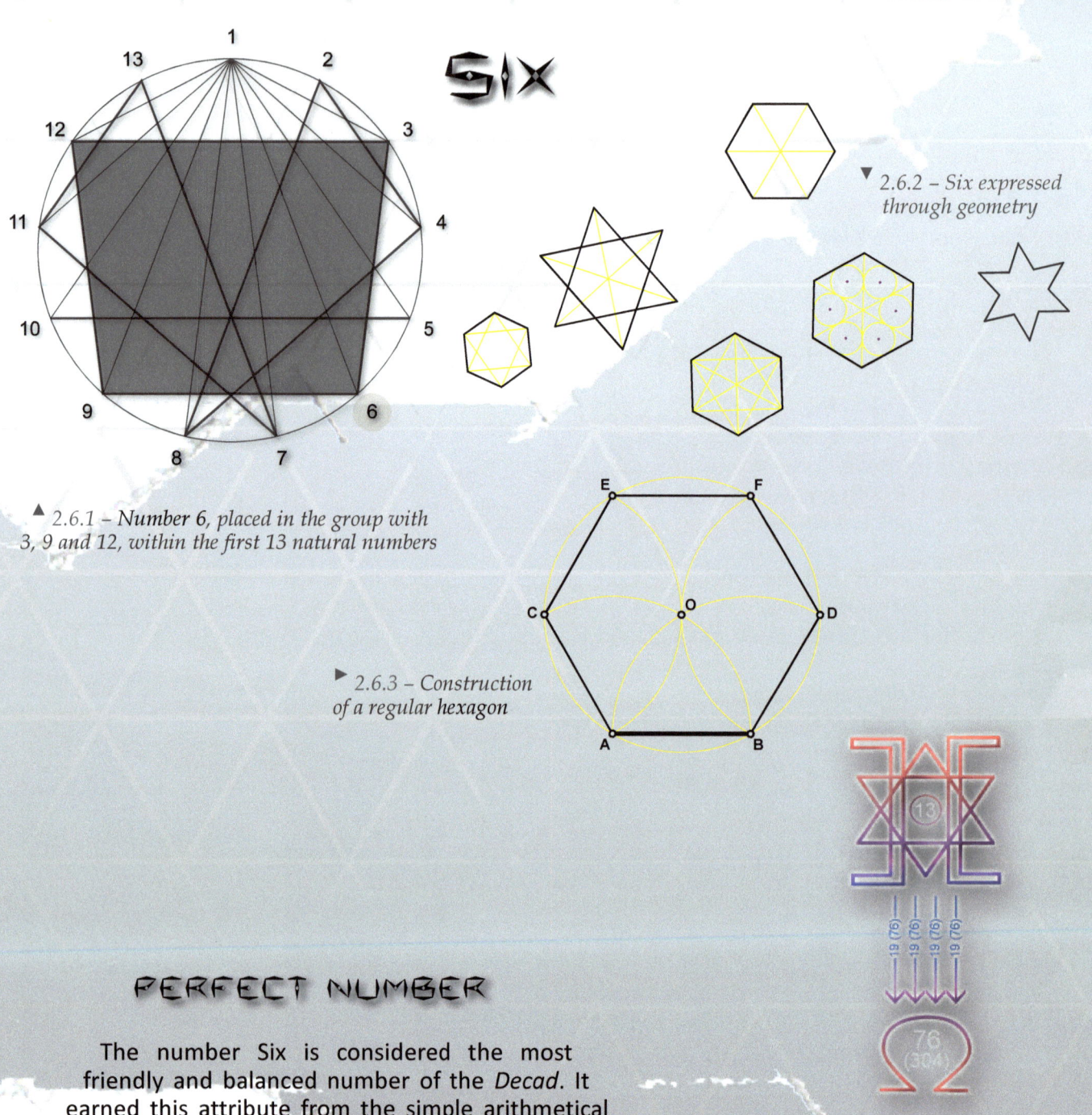

▲ 2.6.1 – *Number 6*, placed in the group with 3, 9 and 12, within the first 13 natural numbers

▼ 2.6.2 – *Six expressed through geometry*

▶ 2.6.3 – *Construction of a regular hexagon*

PERFECT NUMBER

The number Six is considered the most friendly and balanced number of the *Decad*. It earned this attribute from the simple arithmetical facts: 2+2+2=6 and 3+3=6 that show how Six can be expressed as a result of the *odd number* of repetitions of the *even number* Two (3x2=6), or the *even number* of repetitions of the *odd number* Three (2x3=6). This bond of *even* and *odd numbers*, inherent in Six, also makes it stable and balanced.

Six, or the *Hexad* in Greek, is unique in yet another way. The addition and multiplication of its divisors give Six: 1+2+3=6 and 1x2x3=6. The number Six is the only such number. Numbers which are equal to the sum of their proper positive divisors, excluding themselves, are called *perfect numbers*. The first five of these numbers are 6, 28, 496, 8128 and 33550336, and the first four of them were known to the ancient Greeks. **Euclid** (325BC–265BC) found a formula to yield them. Interestingly, every *even perfect number* has Six or Eight as its last digit.

▲ *2.6.4 – Six equal coins conceal five triangles*

The number 28 is, for example, a numerical leitmotif of **Albrecht Dürer**'s self-portrait painted in the year 1500 when he was 28 years old. In the precise way of choosing the measurements of their artwork, and in the setting up the composition of the elements, renaissance masters were subtly encoding the knowledge they possessed. They either intuited, or knew, that shapes were representatives of numbers – being nothing but numbers parading around us in disguise. These artists also understood harmony and the role of proportion. All the knowledge they acquired, they utilised in an implicit way so that it remained a secret only for the ignorant.

Perfect numbers are present in the structure of many codes of nature like, for example, in DNA. In an 8x8 matrix of DNA, the key points of classification are positions 3, 7, and 31 which are the base for the first three *perfect numbers*: 6 (**3**x2), 28 (**7**x4) and 496 (**31**x16). For the fourth *perfect number*, 8128 (**127**x64), the number 127 stands as a base, while the number 64 connects it to the 8x8 matrix.

SIX AND FIVE

Arithmetical insight into Six and Five reveals the common elements between them which are the numbers Two and Three. Their product is six, while five is their sum. Two and Three are representatives of *female* (*even*) and *male* (*odd*) aspects, recognised in the consideration of numbers. In their particular way, Five and Six reconcile these two archetypes. Establishing whether an integer is *odd* or *even* in mathematics is called *specification of its parity*.

The numbers Five and Six have one more thing in common – both numbers maintain self-reference in the result of calculating any power: in the case of Five (5x5=2**5**, 5x5x5x5=62**5**) and in the case of Six (6x6=3**6**, 6x6x6x6=129**6**). This echoing is an attribute of only Five and Six, the trivial example of the number One being ignored.

From the given arithmetical observations related to Six, it is becoming clear why this number is attributed with qualities such as order, balance, wholeness, harmony, symmetry and beauty.

HEXAGONAL GEOMETRY

The Knowledge Book(II-6.1) informs us that the six-pointed star, made by the overlapping of right-side-up and upside-down equilateral triangles, is an emblem of the *focal point of the divine plan* (Fig. 2.6.10). The right-side-up triangle is a symbol of the *training, religious and educational mechanism* of the *divine plan* which the Lord employed to reach human being by introducing Himself through sacred books. This triangle therefore pertains to the religious education and purification that lead to religious fulfilment. Upon completion of that evolutionary programme, when the human being attains a consciousness of one God and belief in Him, the upside-down triangle comes into effect. Hence, the *divine plan* continues to purify the human being, though from this stage through *universal training* on the path of unification with the universal totalities. The aim is for the human being to reach the Lord using personal effort.

The six-pointed star has been widely appreciated around the world by many cultures. The three-dimensional representation of this glyph is a solid known as the star-tetrahedron.

▶ 2.6.5 – *Three, manifesting Six, establishes an infinite communication path of macrocosms and microcosms*

▶ 2.6.6 – *The power and beauty of a trinity*

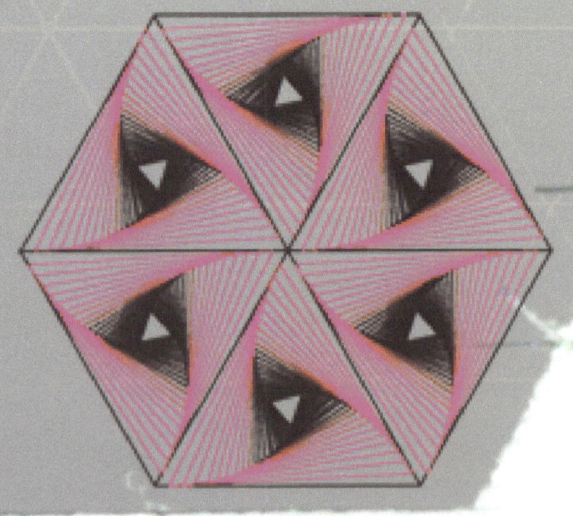

▲ 2.6.7 – *Whirling hexagon – illustration by Sándor Kabai*

In the religions of the Jews, Muslims and Christians, whose sacred books reveal that God created the world in six days, the number Six is regarded as a symbol of perfection and completion. The six-pointed star is a vibrational carrier of that belief in all three of these monotheistic religions. The Jews call it the *Star of David* while an earlier belief considered it to be the *seal of King Solomon*. Common to all these traditions is interpretation of this glyph as a symbol of union between conflicting factors, or of two opposing principles: the earthly (ephemeral) and the celestial (eternal). It has been used extensively in magical, occult and alchemical practices and featured on numerous pieces of art and architecture as an eloquent message for the initiated, since it was attributed with the most magical power of all symbols.

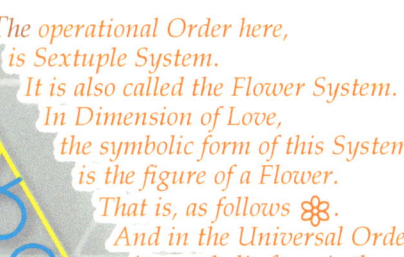

> *The operational Order here,*
> *is Sextuple System.*
> *It is also called the Flower System.*
> *In Dimension of Love,*
> *the symbolic form of this System*
> *is the figure of a Flower.*
> *That is, as follows ✽.*
> *And in the Universal Order,*
> *its symbolic form is the unification*
> *of three triangles on a Focal Point ⛬.*
> *This figure is the Connection System*
> *of a central power to Six Essence Powers.*
>
> *This operational order is the projection*
> *of the operational order of*
> *a Gürz System…*
>
> The Knowledge Book
> (F35, p 576, par 3,4)

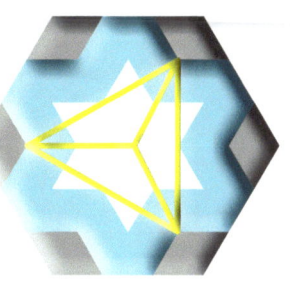

▲ 2.6.8 – The numbers 3, 6 and 18 provide an everlasting organisational pattern

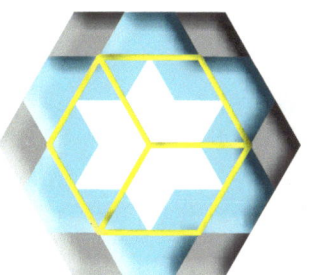

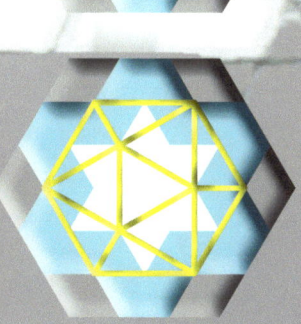

▲ 2.6.9 – Regular solids and the number Six

WHAT AN ASPIRIN AND A SAXOPHONE HAVE IN COMMON

We come across the *Hexad* in many areas of life. It is generally more present in the geometry of forms of inanimate nature like snowflakes, though it is found in living forms as well. As a common denominator, it can even connect a honeycomb with a turtle. For example, Six is present in:

* the number of strings on a *standard guitar,* and the number of basic holes or keys on a *saxophone, clarinet* and *bassoon,* as well as in the number of musicians which form a *sextet;*

* the underlying geometrical structure of many artworks, and architectural elements, like floors, windows, numerous decorations, and in the geometry of altars in sacred buildings;

* the number of legs of animals called *hexapods,* which include insects like *flies, moths, ants, beetles* and *wasps,* and in the geometry of *tortoise* shells, scales on a *fish* and the skin of *reptiles;*

▲ 2.6.10 – The symbol of the focal point of the DIVINE PLAN, that is of the MIGHTY ENERGY focal point[II-6.1]

> *The cause of the six-sided shape of a snowflake is none other than that of the ordered shapes of plants and of numerical constants; and since in them nothing occurs without supreme reason... but such as existed from the first in the Creator's design and is presented from the origin to the day in the wonderful nature of animal faculties, I do not believe that even in a snowflake this ordered pattern exists at random.*
>
> *Johannes Kepler*

* every *cube*, since it has six faces — so another name for a cube is a *hexahedron*;

* the geometry of a *honeycomb*, in a beehive, where the hexagonal structure is the cause of the unusual strength of these creations (Fig. 2.6.14);

* the geometry of many molecular structures, like those of *vitamin C, aspirin, wood cellulose*; crystals like *quartz*, and *artificial crystals*;

* some *flower heads* (Fig. 2.6.15, 2.6.17) as well as in some fruits like *pomegranate* (Fig. 2.6.13)

* the geometry of the *Platonic solids* (Fig. 2.6.9): especially the *octahedron*, which has six vertices, and the *tetrahedron*, which has six edges,

* three-digit *master numbers* (Fig. 2.6.12) since the number 37, present in each of them (3x37=111), as a *figurate number* can take a form both of a hexagon and a hexagram (Fig. 1.5);

* the number of water molecules that are the base of each *snowflake* (Fig. 2.6.11).

> There are no two identical snowflakes, just as there are no two identical human beings. The similarity extends even further: the same as snowflakes, we arrive from the sky.

> Each flower, as well as each snowflake, is a natural mandala.

▲▼ 2.6.11 – *Studies of snow crystals by Wilson Bentley*[II-6.2]

▶ 2.6.12 – *Three-digit Master numbers that relate to the figurate number 37: a) number 111 (222) (37x3=111); b) number 333*

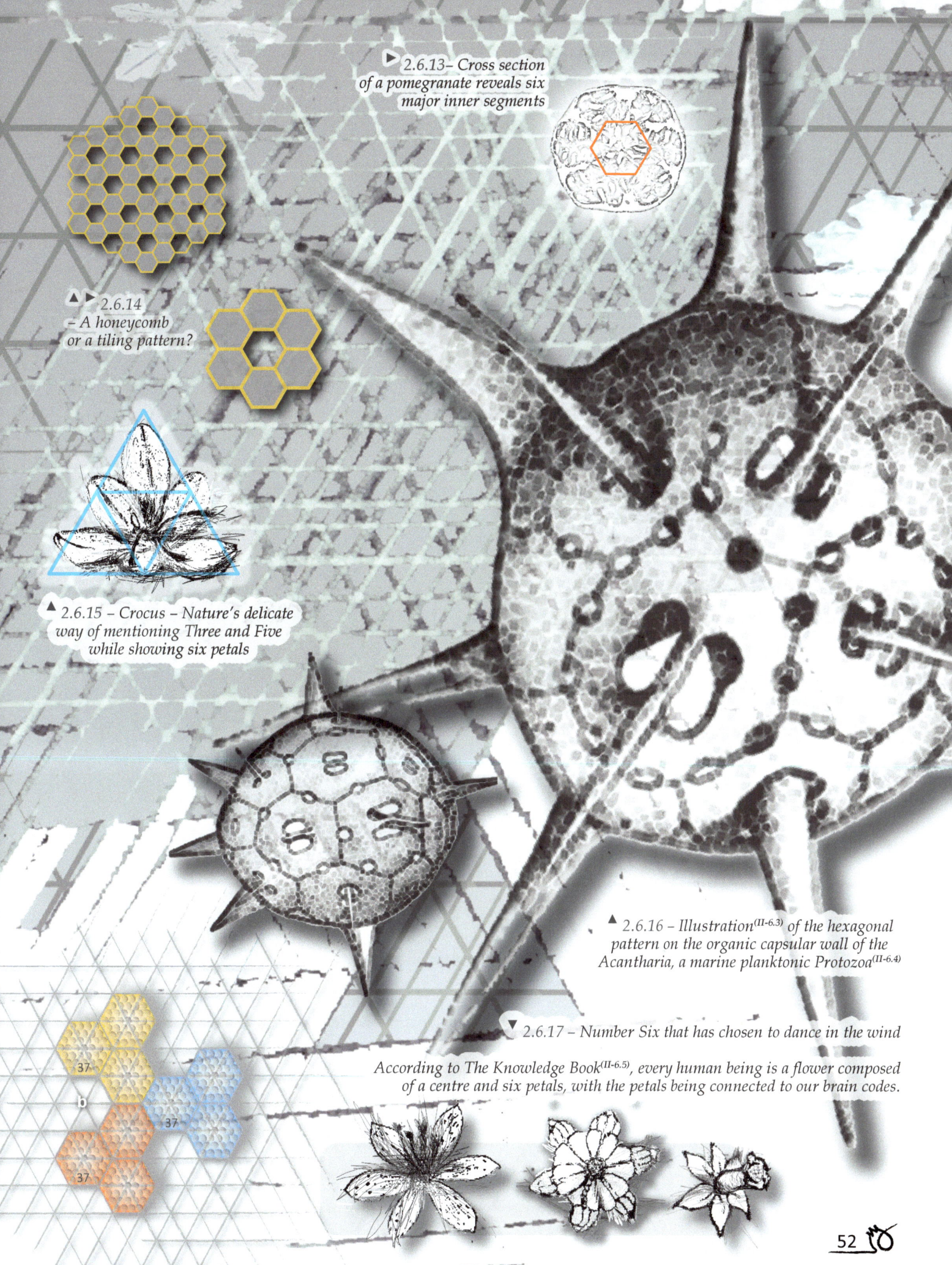

2.6.13 – Cross section of a pomegranate reveals six major inner segments

2.6.14 – A honeycomb or a tiling pattern?

2.6.15 – Crocus – Nature's delicate way of mentioning Three and Five while showing six petals

2.6.16 – Illustration(II-6.3) of the hexagonal pattern on the organic capsular wall of the Acantharia, a marine planktonic Protozoa(II-6.4)

2.6.17 – Number Six that has chosen to dance in the wind

According to The Knowledge Book(II-6.5), every human being is a flower composed of a centre and six petals, with the petals being connected to our brain codes.

NINE

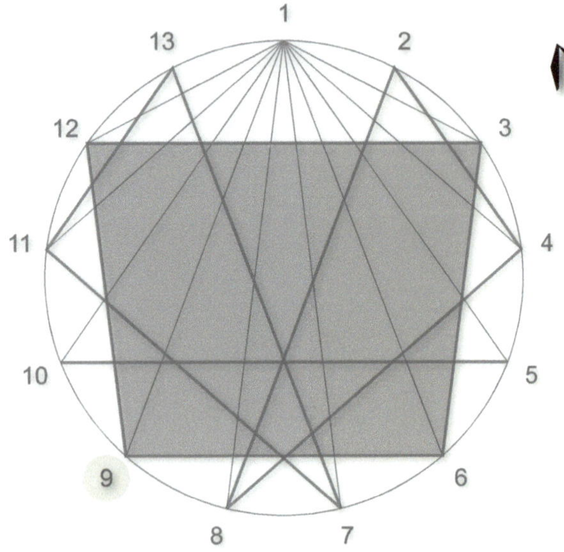

▲ 2.9.1 – *Number 9, placed in the group with 3, 6 and 12, within the first 13 natural numbers*

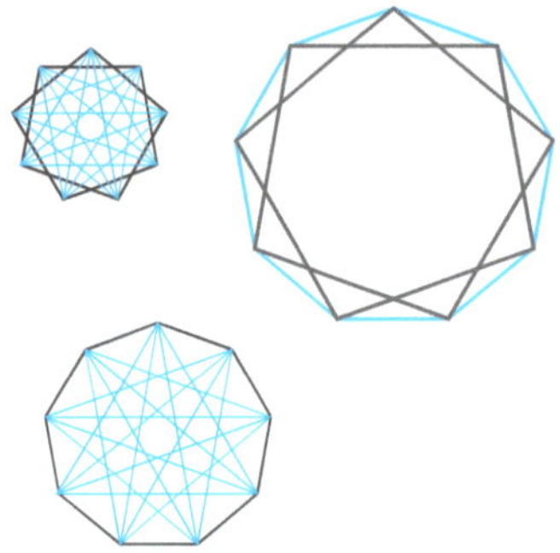

▲ 2.9.2 – *Patterns based on Nine*

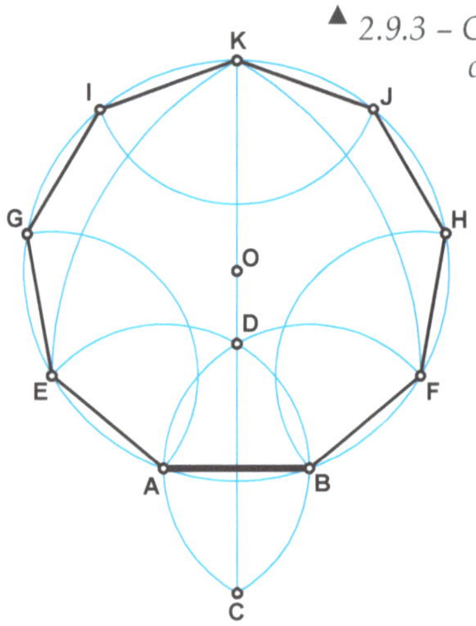

▲ 2.9.3 – *Construction of a nonagon*

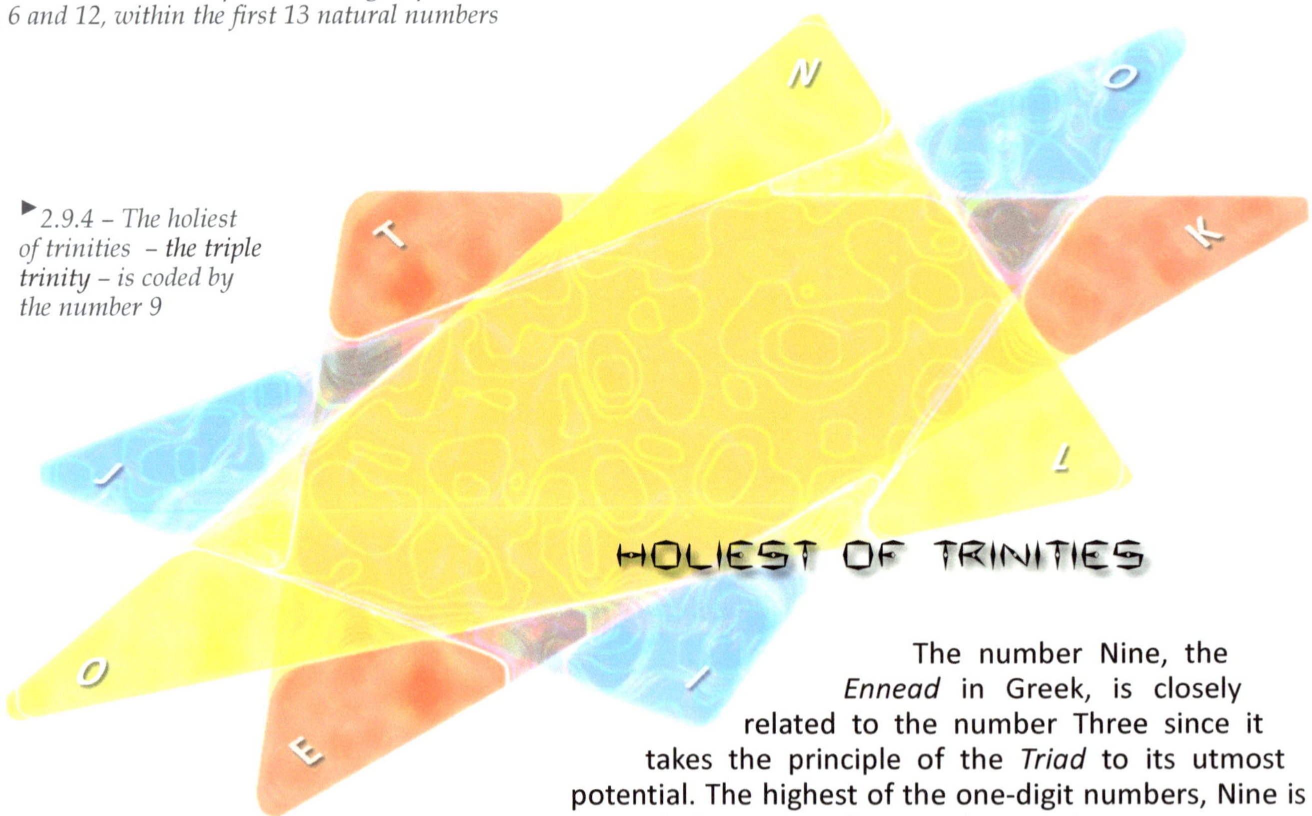

▶ 2.9.4 – *The holiest of trinities – the triple trinity – is coded by the number 9*

HOLIEST OF TRINITIES

The number Nine, the *Ennead* in Greek, is closely related to the number Three since it takes the principle of the *Triad* to its utmost potential. The highest of the one-digit numbers, Nine is 3+3+3 and also 3x3. In these arithmetical operations, we find only the number Three present either as a component, or a divisor, of the number Nine.

Structurally, the number Nine is uniform and clear. As it triples the phenomenon of *trinity*, it is considered three times as sacred. This unique property was recorded and has come down throughout history, and in various cultures, in the *magic square* made of 3x3 small squares.

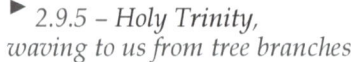

▶ 2.9.5 – *Holy Trinity, waving to us from tree branches*

  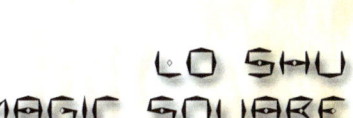

LO SHU MAGIC SQUARE

Lo Shu is the Chinese name for the 3x3 *magic square* that has been present in Eastern magical tradition for more than two millennia (Fig. 2.9.6, 2.9.7). According to Chinese records, the discovery of this *magic square* is attributed to the sage **Yu** who, more than 4000 years ago, saw it on the shell of a turtle arising from the river Lo.

The *Lo Shu magic square* is extensively used in *fengshui* to analyse a house or a site, and for making predictions, and suggestions for changes to the occupants. In the *fengshui* tradition the *Lo Shu* unlocks the time dimension while its central number is considered the reigning number for the relevant time cycle. Every twenty year cycle, as part of the sixty-year interval called an *era*, has its own combination of numbers in the *Lo Shu*. Thus, the movement of the numbers through the various chambers, from cycle to cycle, has a specific meaning.

There are eight different directions for adding the three numbers placed in the chambers of this 3x3 square. Regardless of the direction used, the sum of the three numbers in a line equals fifteen.

In Western tradition, the *magic square* with the same numbers, as in the *Lo Shu,* is considered to be a square of the planet Saturn, or the planet Earth under some circumstances. The zig-zag line, made of a succession of numbers One to Nine, is called the *seal of Saturn* or the *seal of Earth* (Fig. 2.9.7b).

◀▲▼▶ *2.9.6 – Known to men for more than 4000 years, the Chinese Lo Shu is the oldest magic square in the world*

This particular *magic square* contains a symmetrical distribution of *even* and *odd* numbers. In Islamic tradition, a numerical combination of *magic squares* is seen as a translation of the harmony of cosmic order, and therefore as yet another illustration of the divine origin, and significance of numbers and their qualitative values.

◀▶ *2.9.7 – a) The Lo Shu magic square with numbers 1–9 arranged so that adding them together, in eight different directions, each time produces 15 b) In the Western occult tradition, the same square is associated with the planet Saturn. The pattern derived by moving from number 1 to number 9, is also called the Seal of Saturn*

NINE AROUND THE WORLD

Modern belief accepted that there were nine planets in our solar system. The ancient Greeks also recognised nine movable celestial spherical bodies, with each one of them having a carefully appropriated *Muse*. Muses were the daughters of *Zeus* and *Mnemosyne*, and were the patron-goddesses of arts and sciences. They were *Calliope*, chief of the muses, (epic poetry/eloquence – appropriated to the *Premium mobile*, supreme Sphere), then *Euterpe* (lyrical poetry – Mercury), *Polyhymnia* (oratory/sacred poetry – Saturn), *Clio* (history – Mars), *Melpomene* (tragedy – Sun), *Thalia* (comedy/bucolic poetry – Moon), *Terpsichore* (choral songs and dance – Jupiter), *Urania* (astronomy – appropriated to the Starry Heavens) and *Erato* (love/erotic poetry).

The Native Americans talk about nine cosmic levels in their myths: four being above the Earth, four below, and the Earth in between them. The Egyptians often symbolised their Pharaohs by nine bows, while the ancient Chinese considered the number Nine the most auspicious number and structured their social laws, social classes, sacred rites and even pagodas in nine layers. On the ninth day of the ninth lunar month, the Chinese have a festival called the *Double Yang*. It is named after the two Nines of the festival's date which, being *odd* numbers, belong to *Yang*. Christian tradition records nine classes of *Angels*. From the highest, these classes are: *seraphim*, *cherubim*, *thrones*, *dominations*, *virtues*, *powers*, *principalities*, *archangels* and *angels*.

▲ 2.9.8 – *The name of God is the cipher of oneness*

WHAT DOES NINE DO IN SPACE

We will also find the number Nine if we reduce to *digital roots* the numbers (18, 27, 54, 486, 1800, 8748, 18000, 236196, 157464000,) that are behind the organisation of the celestial body called the *Gürz crystal*. Obviously, the number Nine is deeply ingrained in the structure of Space being a *digital root* of all of them.

> Acquiring the digital root of any number is a process of adding up its digits until the result is a one-digit number.
>
> For example, such a digital compression of the number 486 shows that the digital root of the number 486 is 9 (4+8+6=18, 1+8=9).

     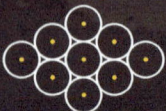

▲ 2.9.9 – *Symmetrical positions of nine equal coins*

*God is sound and silence.
His name is Om.*

*Gautama Buddha
(The Dhammapada*[II-9.1]*)*

HOW MANY NAMES DOES GOD HAVE

The religious books given to humanity have acknowledged 999 names of God[II-9.2]: 300 names in *The Psalms of David*, 300 names in *The Old Testament*, 300 names in *The New Testament* and 99 names in *The Quran*. It has also been suggested that only one of these names is the genuine one and consists of 147 words[II-9.3].

According to *The Knowledge Book* the number Twelve, obtained from the number 147 (1+4+7=12), relates to the fact that the great Prophets had twelve assistants: **Jesus Christ** had twelve *Apostles*, **Mohammed** had twelve *Imams* and **Moses** twelve *Cherubims*. Every letter, of this 147-word-long genuine name of God, symbolises the name and the mission of the Prophets' assistants.

Some names of God revealed in holy books:

HAM – given to Buddha
AUM (OM) – In Indian Vedas
I AM – given to Jesus in The Bible
HA-MIM – given to Mohammed in The Quran
TETRAGRAMMATON – given to Moses in The Bible

MULTIPLYING BY NINE

2+9=11

| | 2x9=18 | 1+8=9 |
| | 9x9=81 | 8+1=9 |

3+8=11

| | 3x9=27 | 2+7=9 |
| | 8x9=72 | 7+2=9 |

4+7=11

| | 4x9=36 | 3+6=9 |
| | 7x9=63 | 6+3=9 |

5+6=11

| | 5x9=45 | 4+5=9 |
| | 6x9=54 | 5+4=9 |

The calculations in figure 2.9.10 show that Nine is the *digital root* of every number which is the product of multiplication by Nine.

The next figure (2.9.11), ensued from the division by Eleven and multiplication by Nine, reveals an intrinsic connection between the numbers Eleven and Nine. The presence of One (as 11) within the operations governed by Nine, shows that Nine never loses its reference to the beginning, to the *Monad*.

▲ 2.9.10 – Multiplying by 9

1:11=0.090909	0+9=9	1x9= 9
2:11=0.181818	1+8=9	2x9=18
3:11=0.272727	2+7=9	3x9=27
4:11=0.363636	3+6=9	4x9=36
5:11=0.454545	4+5=9	5x9=45
6:11=0.545454	5+4=9	6x9=54
7:11=0.636363	6+3=9	7x9=63
8:11=0.727272	7+2=9	8x9=72
9:11=0.818181	8+1=9	9x9=81

▲ 2.9.11 – On relations between Nine and Eleven

19 X 26000

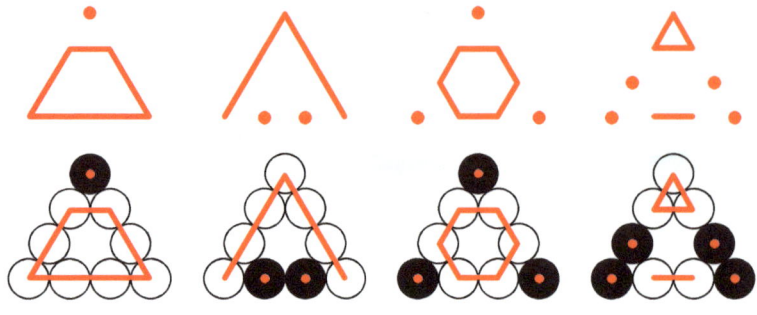

▲ 2.9.12 – *Symmetrical patterns originating from a triangular presentation of Nine as a collection of black and white balls. Patterns are emphasised by the use of dots and lines.*

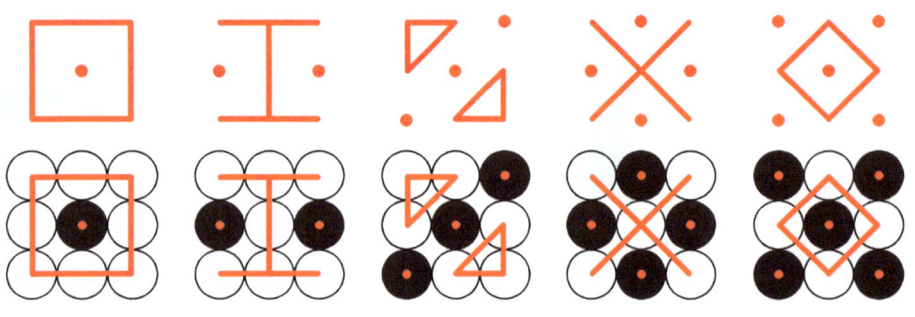

▲ 2.9.13 – *Symmetrical patterns derived from a square presentation of Nine*

> Looking at the patterns in figures 2.9.12 and 2.9.13 we do not immediately associate them with the numbers, which are behind them in the first place. The same is true of all other shapes and patterns – numbers define them.
>
> Numbers are the Spirit's qualitative constants. They illustrate its wisdom in finding the tool to translate its own inherent order and principles, from the world of the intangible, into the world of sound, colour and visible physical form.
>
> Numbers are the universal language of Spirit.

Figures 2.9.12 and 2.9.13 illustrate the simple arithmetic of the right-hand column in figure 2.9.10 and of the middle column in figure 2.9.11. They expose symmetry patterns of the relationship formed by the two numbers that add up to Nine. Symmetry is explored in the triangular and square arrangements of the nine balls, where the pattern determiner is the position of the black and white balls.

BEYOND APPEARANCES – 9X9 TABLE

The familiar 9x9 table (Fig. 2.9.14a) contains some interesting geometrical patterns. They indicate the work of higher dimensions of order behind these simple numerical operations.

To demonstrate, we will calculate the *digital roots* of the numbers in the 9x9 table (Fig. 2.9.14b).

The new version of the 9x9 table, made of *digital roots* only, reveals symmetries that exist in the table and the role the number Nine plays in exposing them (Fig.2.9.15).

1	2	3	4	5	6	7	8	9
2	4	6	8	10	12	14	16	18
3	6	9	12	15	18	21	24	27
4	8	12	16	20	24	28	32	36
5	10	15	20	25	30	35	40	45
6	12	18	24	30	36	42	48	54
7	14	21	28	35	42	49	56	63
8	16	24	32	40	48	56	64	72
9	18	27	36	45	54	63	72	81

a

1	2	3	4	5	6	7	8	9
2	4	6	8	1	3	5	7	9
3	6	9	3	6	9	3	6	9
4	8	3	7	2	6	1	5	9
5	1	6	2	7	3	8	4	9
6	3	9	6	3	9	6	3	9
7	5	3	1	8	6	4	2	9
8	7	6	5	4	3	2	1	9
9	9	9	9	9	9	9	9	9

b

▲ 2.9.14 – *The 9x9 table (a) and its digital roots version (b)*

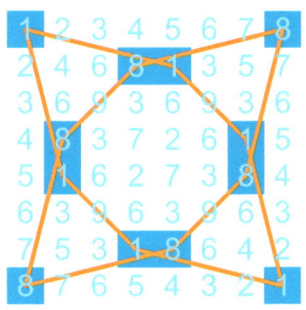  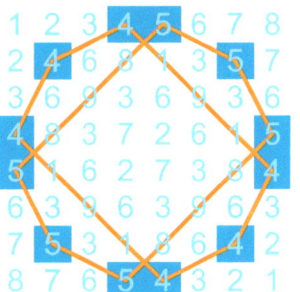 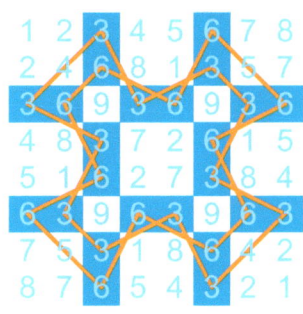

▲ 2.9.15 – *Patterns derived from the pairs of numbers that add up to Nine (1+8, 2+7, 3+6, 4+5), in the digital roots table shown in Fig. 2.9.14b*[II-9.4]

The Ennead "flows around the other numbers within the Decad like an ocean."

Nichomachus of Gerasa[II-9.5]

Numbers that are complementary to Nine, through the way they appear in this table, form geometrical patterns that are either similar or identical but rotated 90 degrees. Therefore, focusing on Nine exposes the geometry behind the order of a 9x9 table.

The results of the multiplication of numbers bigger than Nine, represented by their *digital roots*, reveal the same patterns.

WHAT SEVEN HAS TO DO WITH NINE

The number Nine hosts another geometrical pattern concealed in a seemingly random collection of digits that appear in the division of the number One by Seven (Fig. 2.9.16). In the resulting number (1:7 = 0.142857142857142857142...) we can notice a regular repetition of the numerical series 142857. Furthermore, the all numbers from One to Nine (except Seven), or any other number which is not a multiple of Seven, when divided by Seven has a quotient which produces the same sequence of 142857. If the six digits of this series mark six points on a circle, that has nine regularly distributed points, and we connect those six points in the same order (1→4→2→8→5→7→1...), we obtain the pattern of ceaseless energy flows as within an enclosed circuit.

The pattern that engages six places out of nine, leaves out the three positions which correspond to the numbers Three, Six, and Nine on the circle. By connecting these three points we get a triangle. Hence, the nine-fold assortment is balanced by the properties of the *Triad*. The numbers Three and Six complement each other, while Nine is a resulting place of their harmonious meeting (Fig. 2.9.16).

▲ 2.9.16 – *One of the ways Six and Three complement and balance each other, within the field defined by Nine*

The circle illustrated in figure 2.9.16 is a symbol of One, the *Monad*. As we have seen, the number Seven is used to arithmetically divide number One which has revealed the inherent symmetries and balance between the first nine natural numbers.

RETURNING HOME

The number Nine is the final character in the row of one-digit numbers. When arriving at Ten, a completely different, more complex medium of combinations of the first nine numbers commences. These are so-called multi-digital numbers which open a whole new world able to deal with infinity. However, the base and the potential of the multi-digital numbers spring from the nature and the characteristics of the numbers One to Nine.

Nine months is the period of human pregnancy, a period from conception to being born in a new dimension. This fact loads the number Nine with additional esoteric meaning and thus the number Nine is considered a symbol of returning Home.

Each one of us evolves through nine layers of our own energy dimension. Evolvement through the first seven layers is subject to the *Mechanism of Influences*. Evolvement through the final two layers, on the other hand, depends on our personal efforts and thought power and is to do with reaching our essence and the consciousness of that particular dimension. This relevance of the number Nine, to our evolution through our own energy dimension, has been symbolically woven into many myths and legends around the world. Heroes of these stories often went through nine difficult tasks, or needed nine years to go through challenges, in order to reach the object of their desires and to achieve the seemingly impossible.

The bigger the challenge, the greater the enthusiasm needed to feed perseverance. Each crisis successfully gone through toughens the fearless heroes. This scenario prepares the medium of awakening and advancement of the character through the labyrinth of its own personality. Faith, focusing and patience are eventually awarded. Through an intense social interaction and numerous struggles, a person gains necessary experiences, gets purified and eventually reaches the target.

The Greek goddess **Demeter** searched nine days for her daughter **Persephone**. In *The Iliad* and *Odyssey*, **Homer** (the 8th century BC) tells us that the city of Troy was besieged for nine years, and that **Odysseus** wandered for nine years while trying to return home, to Ithaca.

Whoever brought me here Will have to take me home. – Mevlana Celaleddin-i Rumi

But, what is it we wish for so deeply that arms us for going through these complex nine-step tests? It is our own higher expression as a state of stable resonance of our being with its divine source. It is a desire to return Home, being stimulated by the God's particle present in us. The self that successfully goes through the evolvement of all nine layers of its own energy dimension, deserves to reach essence-God-consciousness and to settle in its own real, everlasting body.

SILVER CORD

Spiritual totality is a mighty energy which neither gets smaller nor bigger, and is eternal(II-9.6). It is an indivisible whole outside our body, and its influence is extended to us through the so-called *silver cord* which connects our brain to it. The Spirit, actually, is not in our body! *Spiritual totality* is beyond dimensions. However, it still reflects on existential dimensions by tailoring its energy intensity. We gradually get used to this invisible energy, and evolution is a programme which serves that purpose. According to its evolutionary age the human being is therefore embodied in a suitable energy medium of a planet, and solar system, and is connected to the *Spiritual totality* in order to complete its own thought evolution.

The 8th evolutionary dimension is called the *Spiritual plan* or *Spiritual dimension*, while the 9th evolutionary dimension is called the *Lordly dimension*(II-9.7) and each of these two dimensions has nine energy layers. Layers of the *Lordly order* are reflected onto the ranks of the *Spiritual plan*. Actual *Spiritual* and *Lordly dimensions*, which are outside the *atomic whole*, cooperate in *Omega dimension*, wherefrom their energy layers are reflected onto the *atomic whole*.

The aim of the evolving human being is to achieve a predetermined genetic perfection. According to its own medium, each solar system has its own evolutionary plan. The lower dimensions are the subject to the influence of the energies from more advanced dimensions crucial for the realisation of that plan. In our solar system, the manifestation of the perfect human being (the 7th evolutionary dimension) takes place at Saturn. The most intensive layers of the 8th and 9th evolutionary dimensions (that is the 9th rank of the *Spiritual plan*, and the 9th layer of the *Lordly order* = the 18th evolutionary dimension) are reflected on Saturn.

Planet Earth is in the 3rd evolutionary dimension, which is the lowest evolvement level in our solar system. That is why it receives reflections from the lowest layers of the 8th and 9th evolutionary dimensions. Energies projected from the *Spiritual plan* we attract by our thought and they initiate the evolvement of the individual, while energies of the *Lordly dimension*, attracted by our cells, supervise that evolvement.

In these observations based on *The Knowledge Book*, we find the number nine within the structure of the *Spiritual* and *Lordly dimensions* which jointly prepare the manifestation of the perfect human being in us.

The Cosmos is an intricate skein. Each Living Entity is obliged to live its Destiny, with its Goodness, its Badness, its Beauty and its Ugliness. Until it is Integrated.

The Knowledge Book
(F14, p 202, par 1)

Without Love, man cannot leave behind his old ways.

Peter Deunov(II-9.8)

TWELVE

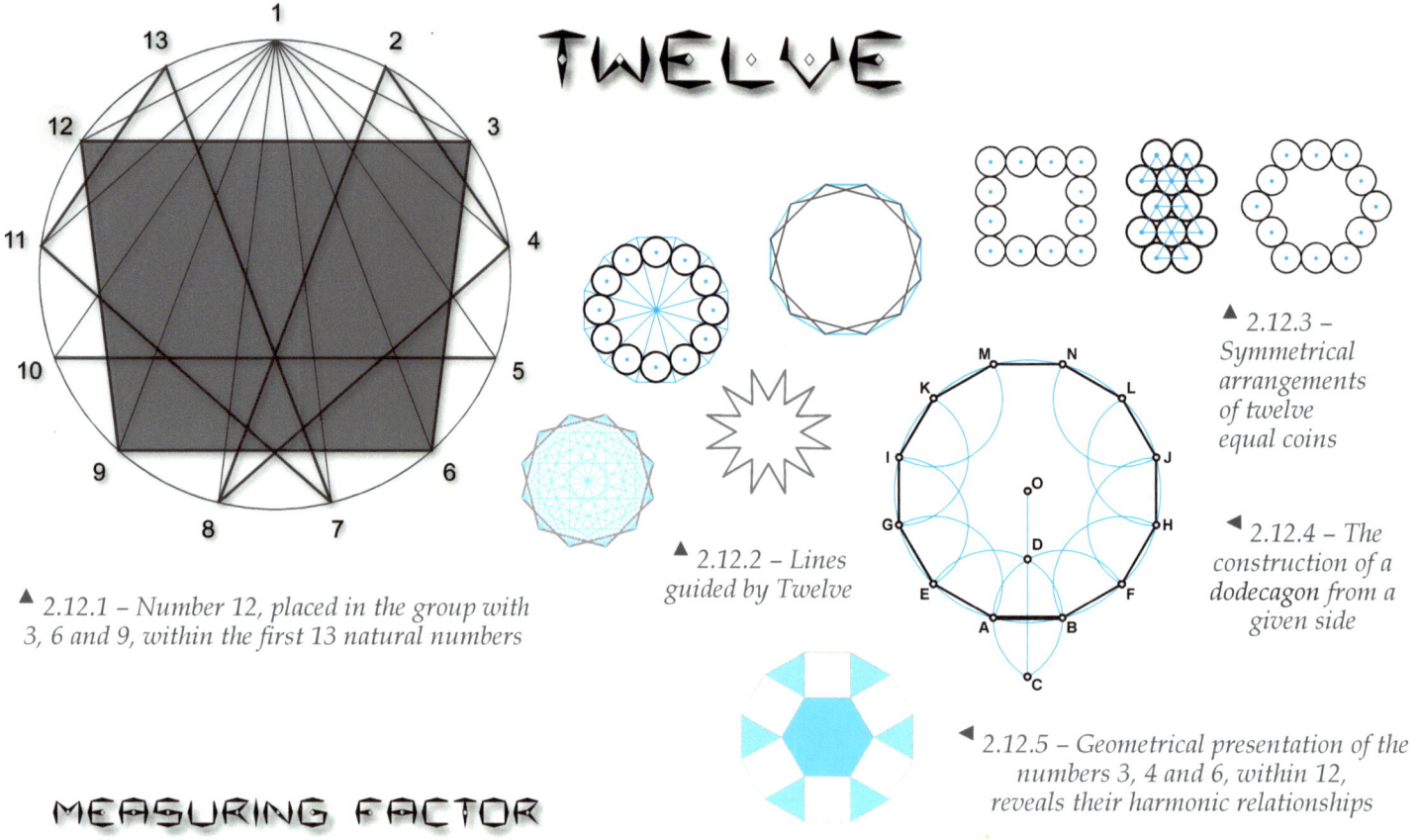

▲ 2.12.1 – Number 12, placed in the group with 3, 6 and 9, within the first 13 natural numbers

▲ 2.12.2 – Lines guided by Twelve

▲ 2.12.3 – Symmetrical arrangements of twelve equal coins

◀ 2.12.4 – The construction of a dodecagon from a given side

◀ 2.12.5 – Geometrical presentation of the numbers 3, 4 and 6, within 12, reveals their harmonic relationships

MEASURING FACTOR

Since ancient times, Twelve has been the number that suggested wholeness and completion. It has also been favoured in various measurements whether they be of time, length or other values. For example, there were twelve pence in a shilling, twelve inches in a foot, and a dozen comprises twelve.

Since 3x4=12, the numbers Three and Four carry their properties into the number Twelve. Islamic cosmological tradition explains the relationship of the numbers Three and Four to the number Twelve through the zodiac. Islamic teachings recognise three principal tendencies of the Spirit *(descending, horizontal expansion* and *ascending)* and four fundamental qualities of universal nature (these are two sets of polarities: *hot-cold* as active, and *moistness-dryness* as passive qualities). All these 3x4 properties work through the twelve signs of the zodiac.

If there is no Life in any other Galaxy than Your World, then how had Your Consciousness, Art, Learning and Your Faith been sown in Your Sub-awareness?

While you solve everything through Your Brain which is a very Perfect Instrument, have You ever Thought, in the Pause of a moment, where do the Codes come from with which that Brain is in contact?

If there are no Living Species living in the Celestial Segments, why did then God create the Living Being in Your Planet and did not create them in other Universes? Was He unable to do so?

If Mankind believes in a Power called God, then they will surely solve the Secret of the Universe in the Consciousness of its own Existence.

If Mankind could Criticize itself in an impartial way instead of arguing in vain about Our existence or non-existence, it could have easily found Us in front of itself.

Your Planet still expects Sounds from the Universe through primitive Radio Signals. But We have gotten in touch with You long ago through Your Radio and TV instruments.

In the Real Realm, We always act within the Telepathic Perceptions of Space. Our conversation is very easy and perfect. Those who are outside this Perception can never establish this communication.

Our Origin comes way beyond Centuries. We are Embodied, We are Loving. If We so desire, We show Ourselves to many Friends and have a conversation. (Like We do with You.) Our technique depends entirely on an Electronic System.

We are not strange Entities, or a Spirit. We are Human Beings just like You. We Breath, We Laugh, We Cry. However, Our Systems are, maybe millions of times more Evolved and Perfect than Yours.

TIME DETERMINANT

Every time we glance at the face of a clock, we connect the context of the self-reflection with the number Twelve. However, that context is a part of a bigger cycle of time structured by Twelve. It is a year with its twelve months. The zodiac, determined by the Sun's passing through the twelve fixed constellations known as the *zodiacal houses,* is also based on the number Twelve.

Terrestrials who come to space cannot see Us. Because, this is a matter of Frequency Adjustment. This adjustment is made to a Frequency on a much Higher Level than the World Frequency. When we harmonize Our Frequency with Yours, We wander about in Your World. Our very difference from You is this.

The Knowledge Book
(F17, p 261, par 2-11)

Completion of one immensely important period of life is marked by the number Twelve. We become teenagers after having lived for twelve years and enter into new programmes of life, leaving childhood behind us. However, that departure is only calendar-wise because childhood experiences continue to live in us.

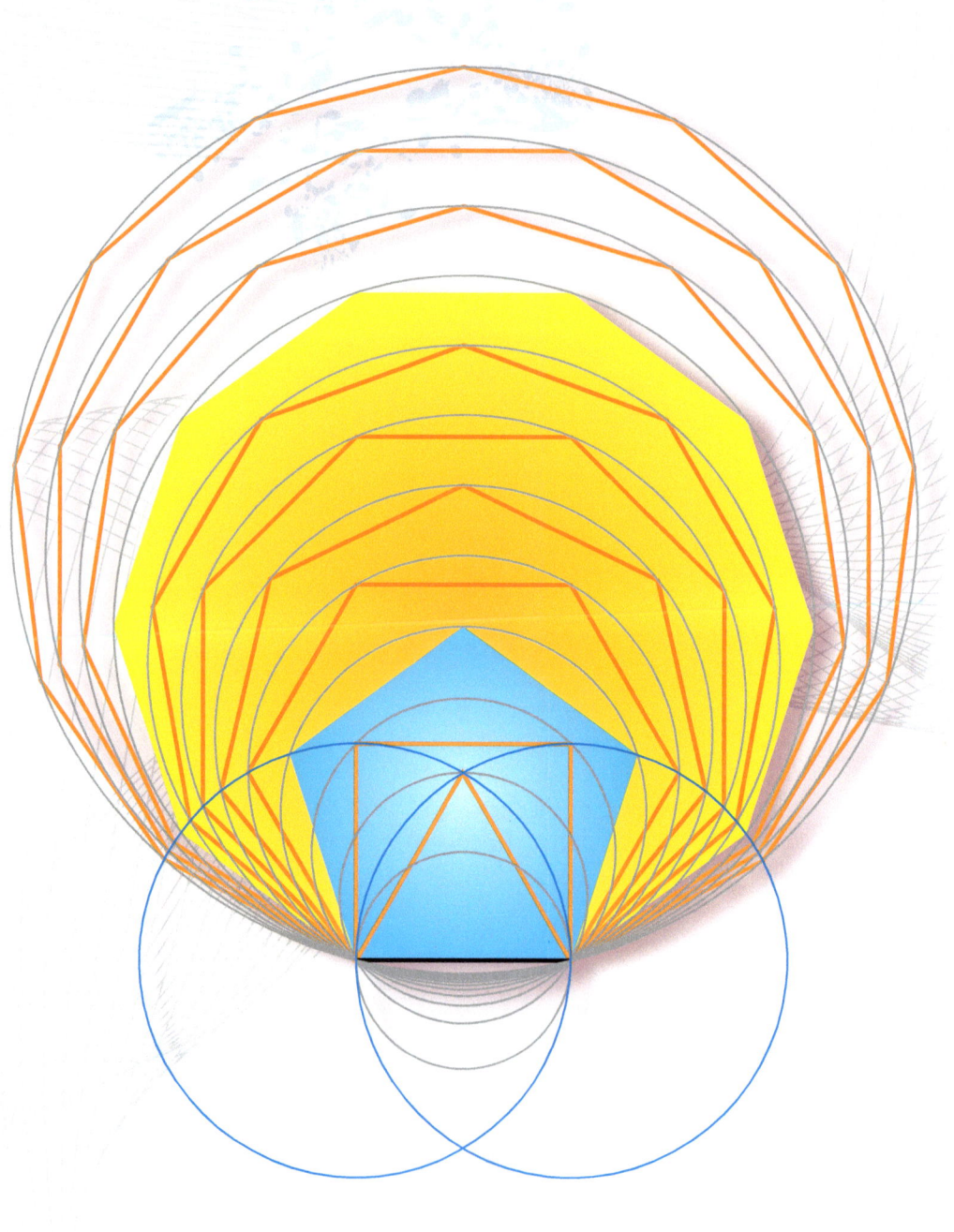

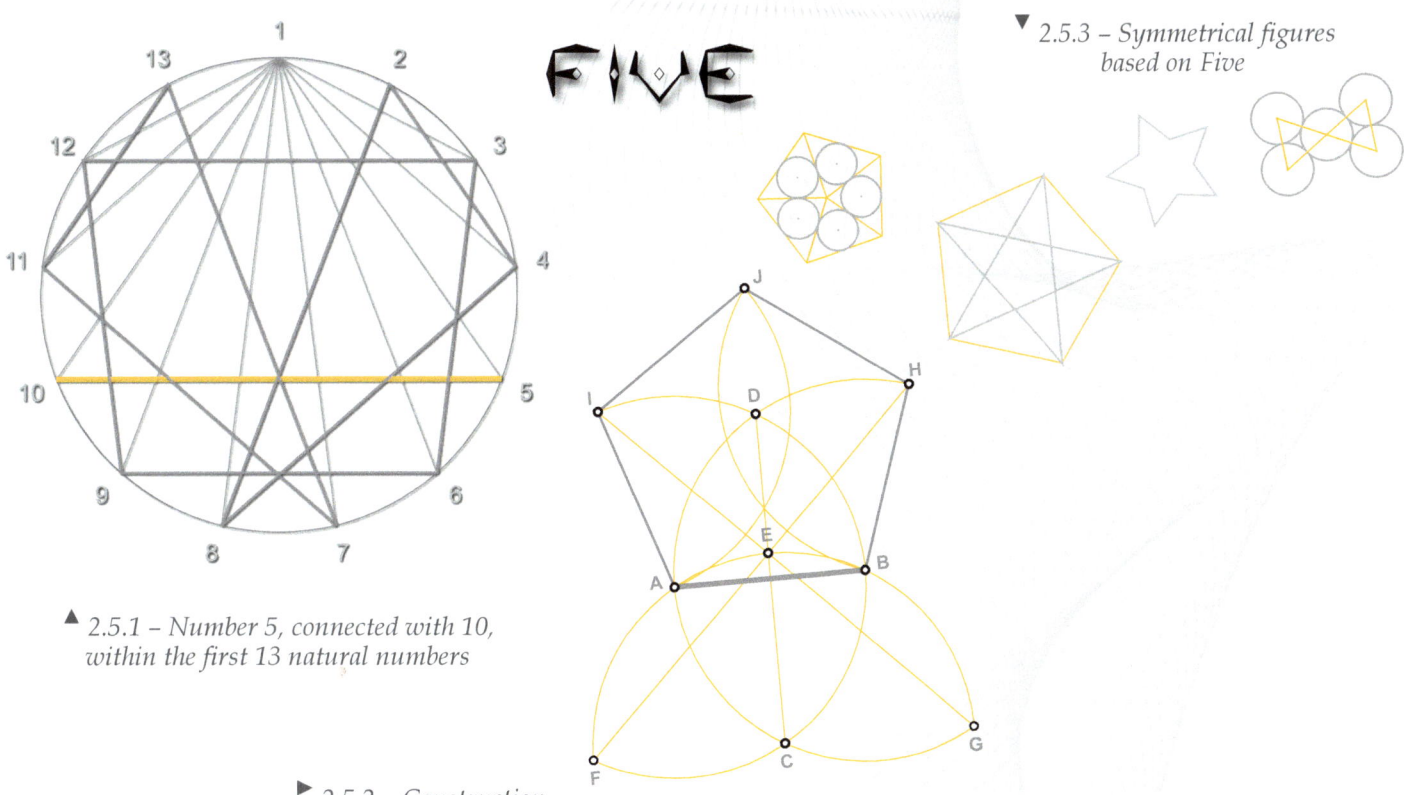

▲ 2.5.1 – Number 5, connected with 10, within the first 13 natural numbers

▶ 2.5.2 – Construction of a regular pentagon

▼ 2.5.3 – Symmetrical figures based on Five

The final Evolution boundary of this Micro Energy is the Human Being. The Body Total of the Human Being, that is, its Biological structure Exhibits an Operational function Equivalent to the Functioning of the Atomic Totality Structure of the Ordinance of Cosmoses. For this very reason, each Human Being is a Cosmos.

Vedia Bülent (Önsü) Çorak
(Light)

BALANCED VIRGIN

Pentad is the Greek word for Five. As the sum of the numbers Two and Three, the number Five is host of an *even, female,* number Two and an *odd, male,* number Three. The number Five embraces them while not allowing a division of itself by any smaller number, keeping itself intact, virgin.

There are five pairs of numbers of the *Decad* that add up to Ten: 1+9=10, 2+8=10, 3+7=10, 4+6=10, 5+5=10. In this series we can observe symmetry in the process of pairing, and notice how it is most explicitly illustrated by 5+5.

The number Five is the half-way point from One to Ten. This gives it attributes of balance and connectiveness.

PENTAGONAL GEOMETRY

The most recognisable symbol of the *Pentad* is a regular five-pointed star, or pentagram. It is an archetypal glyph that has been embedded in our subconscious from where it speaks to us about brilliance, perfection and the highest standards. Even people are called *stars*, when their success has reached an extraordinary level; we use the phrase *the twinkle in our eyes,* when our inner light starts shining after being ignited by genuine excitement.

Since the regular pentagon and pentagram are storehouses of the *golden proportion,* they are geometric instructions for achieving harmony in the world of form (Fig. 2.5.8). Hence, whether they are outside or inside us, through the *golden proportion* ingrained in them these two figures emanate divine order.

The Pythagoreans highly respected the regular five-pointed star and to them it was a symbol of health and humanity. *The Knowledge Book*[(II-5.1)] reveals the cosmic relevance of the five-pointed star as a symbol for the *Directing Mechanism* of the *Unified Reality* (Fig. 2.5.5).

▲ 2.5.4 – The self-reflection of a pentagram through harmonic diminution

▲ 2.5.5 – The pentagram – a symbol of the Directing Mechanism of the Unified Reality[(II-5.1)]

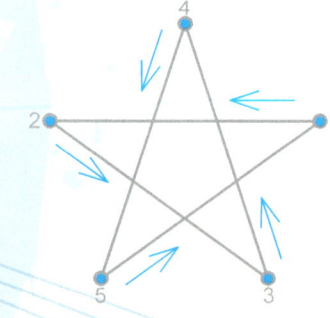

> One who remembers the self (like the smaller stars becoming aware of their own shape, in Fig. 2.5.6) evokes the shape of the self-similar Initial Star (God) thus activating its own godly essence.
>
> Godly I AM Totality of Infinite Awareness echoes through all smaller stars as their individual I AM awareness.
>
> The Self is a wholeness of God and a fragment which reflects His properties.

▲ 2.5.6 – Initial , the biggest star, spread through its own body in the golden proportion

▲ 2.5.7 – *Each of these leaves shows the number Five in a unique way*

FIVENESS AND HUMAN BODY

The organic world flourishes through the principle of the *Pentad*. We can witness it in humans, plants and many animals displaying pentagonal symmetry.

Two arms, two legs and the head of a human body, as five limbs, indicate pentagonal structure. When we stretch our arms and place our legs well apart, our body resembles the form of a pentagon (Fig. 2.5.12). We also have five senses: *smell*, *taste*, *sight*, *touch* and *hearing* while the world we live in comprises five realms: *mineral*, *plant*, *animal*, *human* and *angelic* in an environment made of five elements: *earth*, *water*, *fire*, *air* and *ether*.

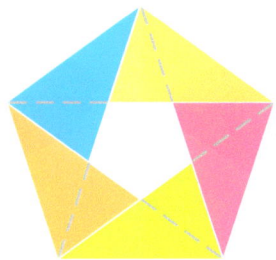

▲ 2.5.8 – *A regular pentagon is a repository of golden triangles*[II-5.2]

◀ 2.5.9 – *Mikhael Ivanov*[II-5.3] *suggests drawing a regular pentagram with movements of our right hand in the air, every night before we go to sleep. Ivanov believed profound properties of its geometry would have healing effects.*

The number Five is an inhabitant of Ten, but Ten is present in Five as well. The fingers on our hands add up to Ten and that is one of the ways the human body makes use of a *Pentad-Decad* relationship. The pentagon is also found in the molecular structure of nitrogen bases *(adenine* and *cytosine)* within the DNA molecules – so, the number Five is present in the very cipher of our biological form.

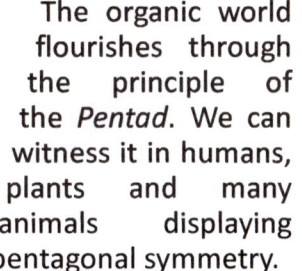

◀ 2.5.10 – *Pentagrams disguised in an apple and star fruit – only a cross section reveals them*

▶ 2.5.11 – *Flower heads – a display of organic pentagonality*

KARENA, the 5th evolutionary dimension, is a preparation stage for being born into the 6th evolutionary dimension called the *dimension of immortality* or NIRVANA.

Period in Karena is equivalent to the period of nine months and ten days of human pregnancy. This dimension one cannot enter with a biological body. We enter it as pure energy, with the eye of our essence visible through our light body made of colours.

In two *tranquil times* of Karena we receive incombustible energies, to enable us to evolve on the planets before the asteroid zone. Then, in five *supreme times* of this dimension, our light foetus is engrafted with the dimensional energies of the planets after the asteroid zone. This energy reinforcement and transformation result in the birth of our everlasting biological body suitable for the *dimension of immortality* and beyond.

As an innermost constituent of our physical body, fiveness is deeply understood by humans and hence our lasting attraction to the regular pentagon and pentagram. Each time we encounter them, endlessness whispers to us through the waves of the *golden proportion* embedded in these forms.

The correspondence of our geometry, be it of a physical, mental or emotional origin, to the geometry in our environment enables the resonance to take place. As a meeting of likes, the resonance is always joyous.

Regular pentagonal geometry acts as a subliminal reminder of our divine origin.

During this Period, Your primary Duty is to recognise Yourselves, to know Yourselves. You are God, You are an Awareness of Universe and a Consciousness. Everything is Concealed in You. During this period, Mankind is becoming the first spark ITS LORD had created. And this Human Being who sits on the throne of Consciousness way beyond Religions will, one day, be the Sovereign of the entire Universe.

The Knowledge Book
(F15, p 223, par 9)

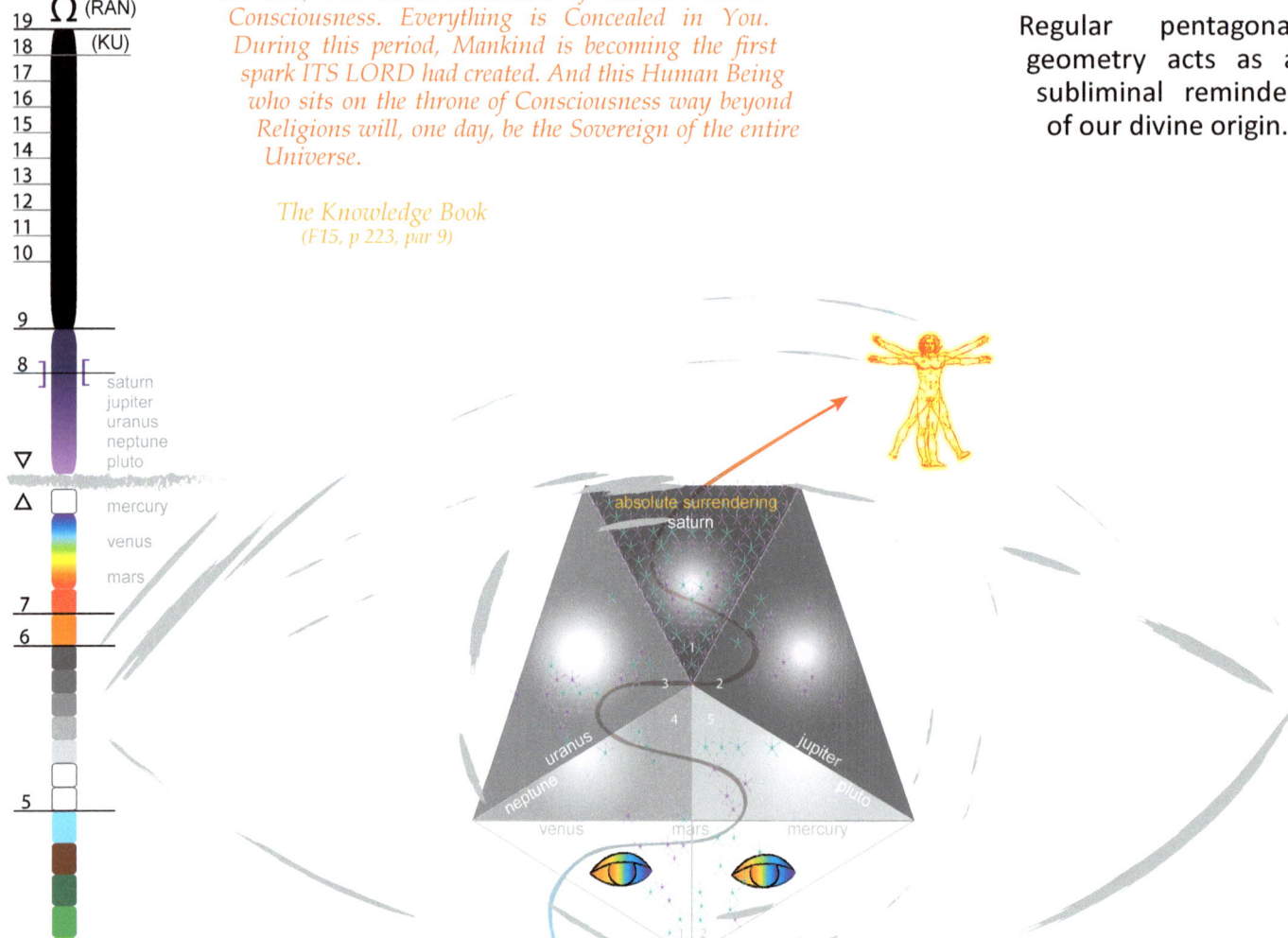

▲ 2.5.12 – *The colour scale of the evolutionary dimensions*[II-5.4]

TEN

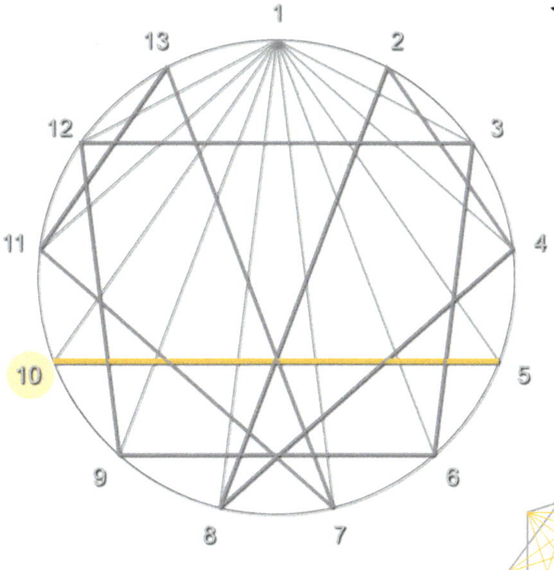

▼ 2.10.2 – Patterns ordered by number 10

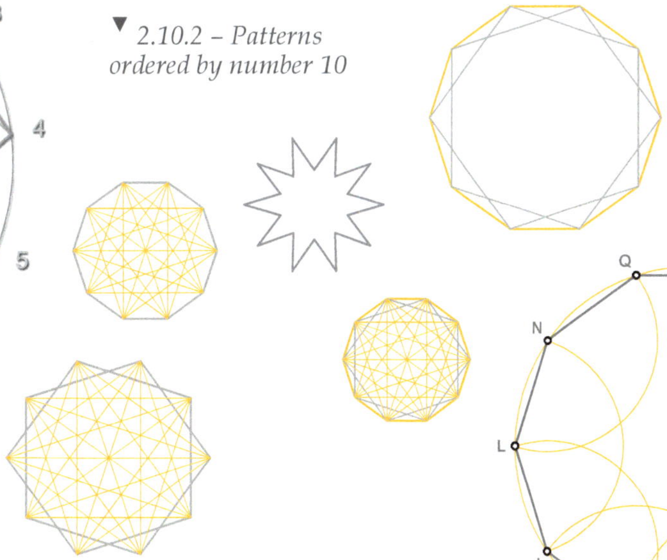

▼ 2.10.3 – Construction of a regular decagon

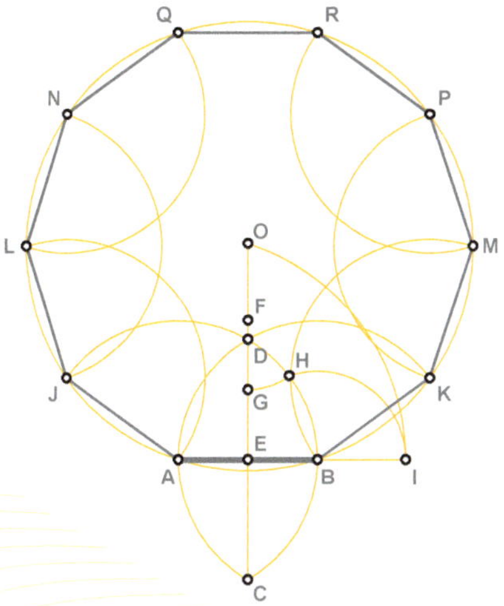

▲ 2.10.1 – Number 10, connected to 5, within the first 13 natural numbers

The Human soul is accustomed to count in Tens.

Johannes Kepler

ENTERING A HIGHER LEVEL OF THE SELF

Through its digits, 1 and 0, the number Ten speaks of absolute presence and absolute absence, of the measurable and the immeasurable. Presence is constantly challenged by absence, as is finite within infinite. Standing side by side in the number Ten, these opposite principles credit the number Ten with great achievement.

Life gradually exposes us to energies of higher intensity, meaning and knowledge. In order to sustain our own existence we need to keep intensifying ourselves. That principle is captured by the number Ten, or the *Decad*.

The number Ten represents the number One entering a higher level of the self, after completing nine steps. It is a symbol of a new phase of living, of a new beginning when the *Monad*, having embraced the challenges of the unknown, makes a shift by embracing a more experienced self. The number Ten is a new unity achieved by living through the nine archetypal principles in a given cycle. It stands for One that marries its own self in a feeling of trust, fulfilment, and readiness for new growth. Ten is One, matured and eager to move forward.

▲ 2.10.4 – Arrangements of ten equal coins

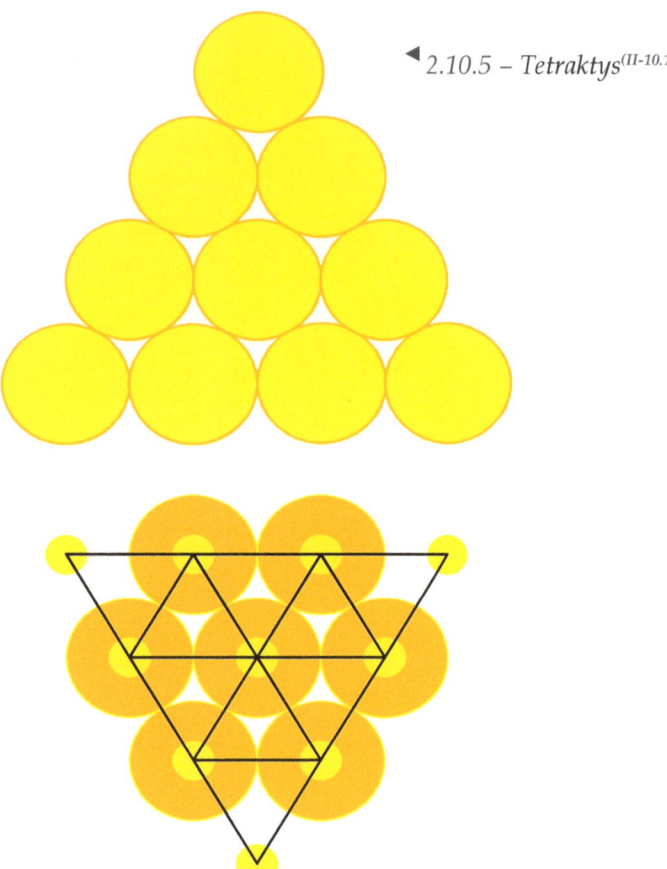

◀ 2.10.5 – Tetraktys*(II-10.1)*

▲ 2.10.6 – A *tetraktys* is a matrix made of ten dots. They determine thirteen triangles (9 smaller and 1+3 larger equilaterals)

A prayer of the Pythagoreans was an address to the *tetraktys*:

*Bless us, divine number, thou who generated gods and men!
O holy, holy Tetraktys, thou that contains the root and source of the eternally flowing creation! For the divine number begins with the profound, pure Unity until it comes to the holy Four; then it begets the mother of all – the all-comprising, all-bounding, the first-born, the never-swerving, the never-tiring holy Ten, the keyholder of all.*

TETRAKTYS

The Pythagoreans regarded the *Decad* highly, and saw all of cosmology encoded in this number. Their favouring of Ten was illustrated by the *tetraktys* (Fig. 2.10.5; 1.1), a figure with a particular choice and order of numbers summed up to Ten: 1+2+3+4=10. This glyph, sometimes called the *mystic Tetrad,* was discussed in chapter ALL IS NUMBER, where it was shown how the ancient Greeks were used to philosophy through numbers. They looked at these ten dots of the *tetraktys* as to an eternal fecundator of all Creation, because they believed it contained patterns of basic creative principles, and secrets of harmonies that are present throughout existence. In *tetraktys* Pythagoreans saw the link between this world and the absolute.

The Tetraktys (also known as the decad) is an equilateral triangle formed from the sequence of the first ten numbers aligned in four rows. It is both a mathematical idea and a metaphysical symbol that embraces within itself – in seedlike form – the principles of the natural world, the harmony of the cosmos, the ascent to the divine, and the mysteries of the divine realm. So revered was this ancient symbol that it inspired ancient philosophers to swear by the name of the one who brought this gift to humanity – Pythagoras.

ascribed to Iamblichus*(II-10.2)*

> *Thought, in fact, is an Energy beyond Matter. You come into Existence by it. However, it is not an Energy You know. Each person's Thought key is concealed in his/her Cerebral Computer. Your Thoughts are operated by gaining speed from the Potential Power here.*
>
> The Knowledge Book
> (F29, p 453, par 1)

Just as it was to the Greeks, the number Ten is very significant to Jews. It is present in the *tree of life* which is their symbol of the highest cosmic and human principles. Both of these cultures assigned to the number Ten a supreme role in translating harmonies of intangible worlds to the physical world of visible forms in which we live. *Above* is reflected *below*, and the miracle of *All That Is* experiences itself in both worlds simultaneously maintaining the overall balance.

Today, the most commonly used number system is based on Ten, having replaced one based on Twelve. To accommodate this seemingly simple numerical change, many different viewpoints were required, for numbers are more than just quantitative factors in our life.

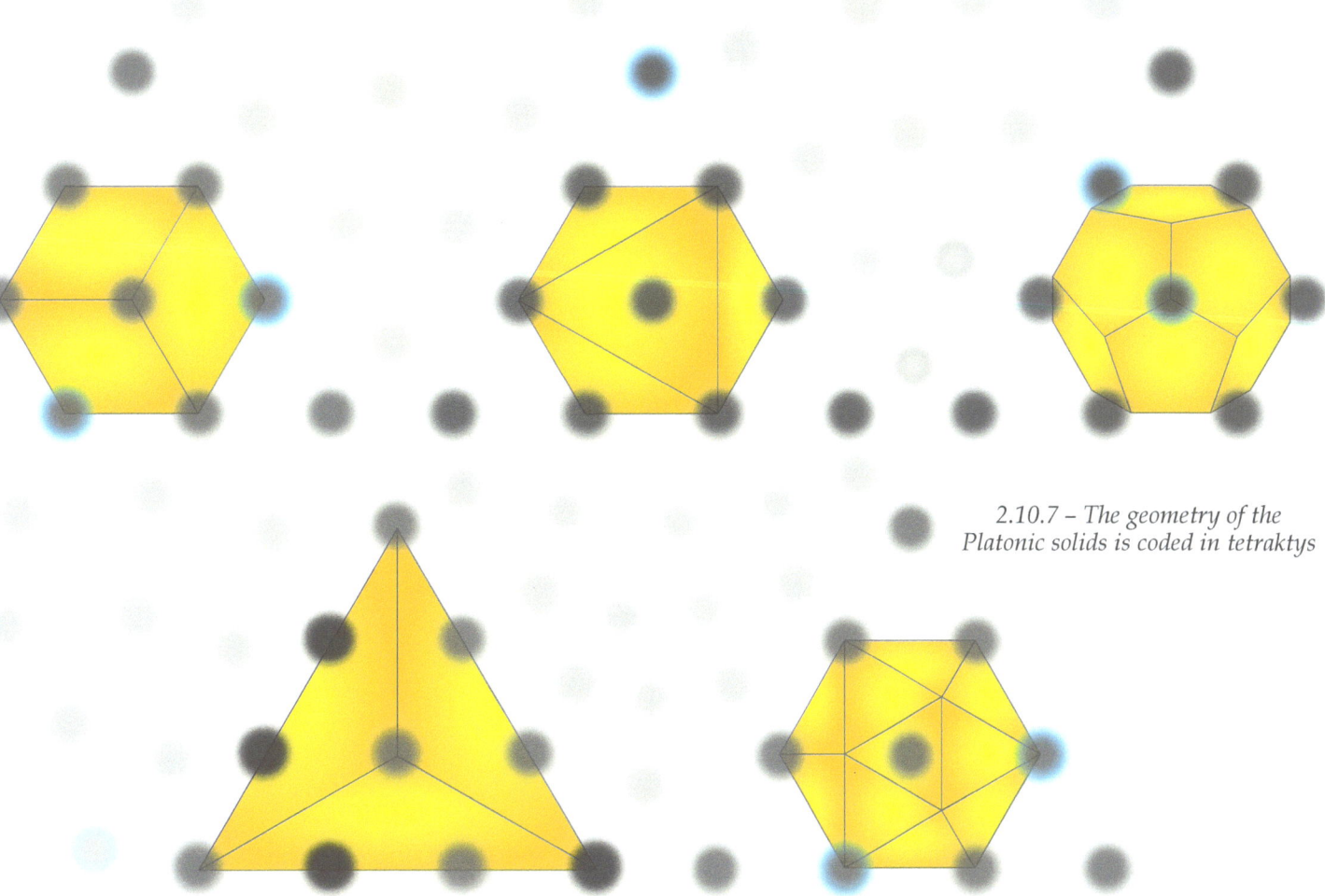

2.10.7 – The geometry of the Platonic solids is coded in tetraktys

SEVEN

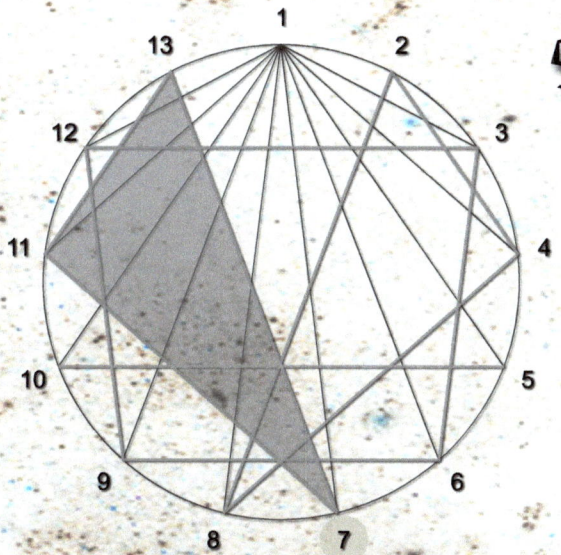

▲ 2.7.1 – Number 7, placed in the group with 11 and 13, within the first 13 natural numbers

▲ 2.7.2 – Some shapes Seven can turn into

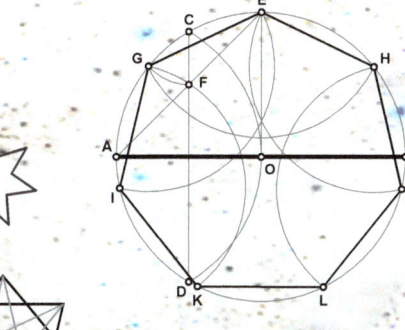

▲ 2.7.3 – Construction of a regular heptagon

MEMORY OF ETERNITY

The number Seven is called the *Heptad* in Greek. It is a *prime number* so it has no divisors within the *Decad* (except the number One and itself). We cannot successfully use a *vesica pisces*, or any of the usual tools of a geometer, to construct it geometrically. Seven requires more precise measuring and yet stays elusive and uncapturable.

The division 360°:7=51.428° shows that the value of the central angles of a regular heptagon is not a whole but a decimal number. On the other hand, the central angles of all other regular polygons within the *Decad* are extracted from 360 degrees without remainder: triangle – 120°, square – 90°, pentagon – 72°, hexagon – 60°, octagon – 45°, nonagon – 40° and decagon – 36°.

The heptagon does not comply with this standard because, among the family of the regular polygons within a *Decad*, it is the only one that holds the memory of infinity while it appears in the world of the finite. The role of Seven seems to remind us of irrational values, rather than to demonstrate inclusiveness or genuine belonging.

2.7.4 – Powers of the colours of the rainbow[(II-7.1)]

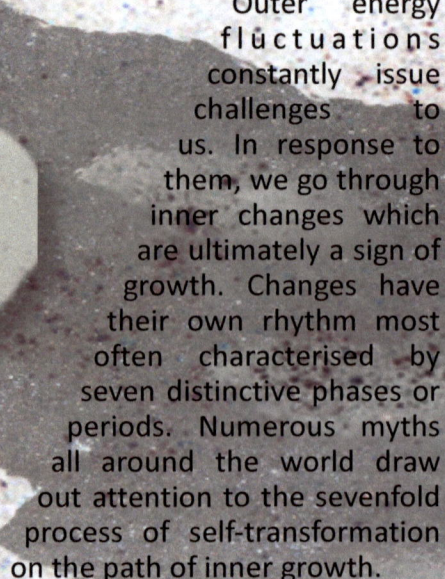

Outer energy fluctuations constantly issue challenges to us. In response to them, we go through inner changes which are ultimately a sign of growth. Changes have their own rhythm most often characterised by seven distinctive phases or periods. Numerous myths all around the world draw out attention to the sevenfold process of self-transformation on the path of inner growth.

2.7.5 – The perfect human being is attained by evolving through three stages of energy/knowledge (terrestrial, celestial and universal) wherein each one has seven layers. The final step of this path in our solar system takes place on Saturn (the 7th evolutionary dimension$^{(II-7.2)}$). Prior to that, a necessary spiritual and cellular transformation in the 5th evolutionary dimension (Karena) gives birth to our genuine immortal body, made of seven layers, which we use from the 6th evolutionary dimension (Nirvana).

FROM THE MIDPOINT IN THE DECAD TO THE MOON

Arithmetically, the number Seven holds a peculiar mid position within the *Decad*: 1x2x3x4x5x6x7=7x8x9x10=5040. If Seven is omitted, an equation still exists and that is: 1x2x3x4x5x6=8x9x10=720. Whether present or not, Seven can be seen as a connector and a divider at the same time.

By expanding on this, if we calculate 8x9x10x11=7920 we get the value of the diameter of the Earth in miles. The significance of the *master number* Eleven in the Earth's radius (720x11=7920) is illustrated through yet another arithmetical operation: 7920/2=3960=360x11. It is interesting that 5040 minus 3960, the radius of the Earth, equals 1080 (360x3=1080), which is the radius of the Moon in miles. Incidentally, the sum of the corner angles of an octagon is 1080 (8x135).

All these numbers, which have been mentioned (7920, 5040, 3960, 1080, 720 and 360), can be reduced to the number Nine as their *digital root*. This kind of analysis, revealing inherent connections within all Creation and its infinite unity ordered through the properties of numbers, seems to have no end.

The number Seven is related to the Moon or, shall we say, the Moon influences our lives through the properties of Seven. A division of the 28-day cycle of the Moon, into its four natural phases, gives seven days to each of these periods called a *week*. The *perfect number* 28 can be seen representing the 28 *houses of the Moon*. In Islamic tradition, each one of them is connected with one letter of the Arabic alphabet.

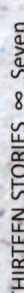

SEVEN - TWELVE RELATIONSHIP

From the equations 3+4=7 and 3x4=12 we see how Seven and Twelve can both be expressed with the use of the numbers Three and Four only (Fig. 2.7.6). Another case of the Seven and Twelve relationship is enabled through the number Five. It can be illustrated by a twelve-note chromatic musical scale, which has seven main tones accompanied by their five *sharp* or *flat* variations.

The astrological significance of the number Seven is captured in the Jewish seven-branched candlestick known as the *menorah* (Fig. 2.7.8). The seven branches represent the orbits of the seven celestial bodies (Sun, Moon, Mercury, Venus, Mars, Jupiter and Saturn) known at the time when the menorah was first made. Related to the twelve houses of the zodiac, these seven celestial spheres also illustrated the relationship between the numbers Seven and Twelve.

The *Seven Heavens*, in Islamic cosmology, was a metaphorical expression related to the seven known planetary bodies which were seen as aspects of the divine intelligence and a bridge between the universal and the earthly.

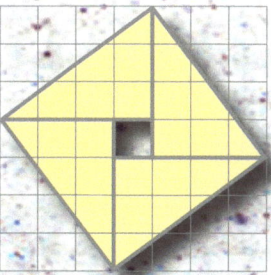

▲ 2.7.6 – 7x7 matrix is the ideal background for the Pythagorean triplet 3-4-5 and for exposing a geometrical relationship between 7 and 12 (4x3). This geometry is found in the Chinese text Chou Pei Suan Ching written between 500BC and 200BC

▼ 2.7.7 – The seven colours of the rainbow

And We have created above you seven paths, and We are never unmindful of creation.

The Quran (23:17)

*Your true home is the seventh stage of spiritual growth, Illiyyun, Reached through purification and peacefulness.
There, you are still in your body, And yet a living Master of the Essence.*

Mevlana Celaleddin-i Rumi

Seven colours of the rainbow embellish the sky on some rainy days. The same colours are associated with seven, out of twelve, major chakras of the subtle human energy body. The word *chakra* is Sanskrit for *wheel* and refers to the energy centres within our body and its energy field, where perpetual exchanges between our energy and cosmic energy take place. Each chakra is also seen as a form of the divine consciousness that descended into these transformation points to govern corresponding bodily functions. Thus the celestial influx of energy keeps our body going, as long as the chakras are open to allow an unobstructed flow. A healthy body is a rainbow of vibrant colours defined by the bundle of our frequencies.

Do you not see how Allah has created the seven heavens, one above another, and made the moon therein a light, and made the sun a lamp?

The Quran (71:15-16)

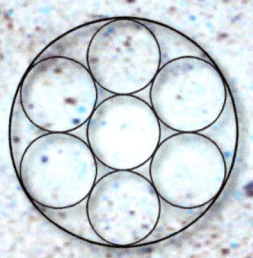

◂ 2.7.9 – The perfect seal – seven equal circles take 77% of the area of the big circle, into which they are placed

▲ 2.7.8 – The Jewish candlestick called menorah

PERFECT SEAL AND ARCHANGEL MICHAEL

Figure 2.7.9 illustrates an inherent property of the circle: every circle conceals seven circles of the same radius inscribed within it in a regular pattern. In esoteric literature, that particular glyph is called the *perfect seal*. *Seven-in-One*, *Seven-as-One* or *Six-around-One* relations have a common geometrical pattern which can be considered a bridge between One and Many. If Seven is the number of people in the group, this pattern enables an efficient connection/communication between them and the Source[II-7.3] (Fig. 2.7.12).

▲ 2.7.10 – *Evolvement of the perfect seal*

The connection between the *perfect seal* and hexagram, obtained from two overlapping equilateral triangles and known in some cultures as the *Seal of Solomon*, is organic (Fig. 2.7.10). The upward-pointing triangle represented the realm of Nature and the ephemeral, while the downward-pointing triangle represented the realm of the Eternal. These two macrocosmic power realms oppose one another in an everlasting interplay and also manifest at the level of the microcosm. The significance of the *Seal of Solomon* was immense in alchemical tradition and, possibly, the *perfect seal* was introduced with the intention of concealing the *Seal of Solomon*.

The inner circle of the *perfect seal* is the quintessence of the six peripheral circles. It was also associated with the **Archangel Michael**, while the six outer circles stood for the six other Archangels. It was believed that the Archangels were related to the seven celestial bodies known at that time, and since **Michael** was the Archangel of the Sun, in the symbolism of the *perfect seal* he was granted the central circle. The *perfect seal* was often represented as a flower, and thus every six-petal flower head is reminiscent of this glyph.

There are many paintings, sculptures and architectural works of the medieval period that feature the *perfect seal* as, for example, the central part of the labyrinth in Chartres Cathedral, in France.

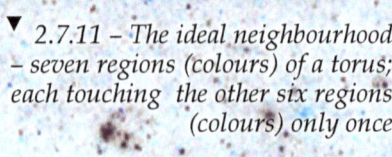

▼ 2.7.11 – *The ideal neighbourhood – seven regions (colours) of a torus; each touching the other six regions (colours) only once*

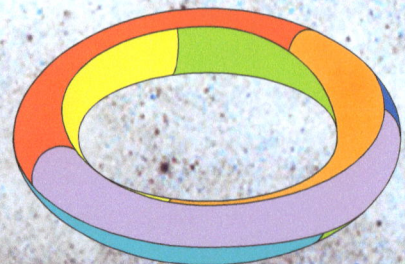

SEVEN COLOURS OF TORUS

The number Seven is related to the *torus*, a shape known to mathematicians as a hypersphere (a sphere with more than three dimensions). Not only does a sweet doughnut have that form but so too do apples, rubber inflated tyres, the magnetic field, tornadoes, whirlpools and galaxies. Cosmologists, who unify relativity with the quantum theory, use the torus shape to describe the universe. Since the surface of the torus can be rotated through its centre in two directions, inwardly and outwardly, they see the torus as a perfect model for black and white holes, as well as wormholes, in the universe (Fig. 2.7.21).

▲ 2.7.12 – *A focal point made of seven subjects provides for efficient horizontal and vertical information flow. Thus, it serves as a perfect reflection network*[(II-7.3)].

Even though it is a space-time construct, the torus can be traced back to its two-dimensional aspect – a rectangle (Fig. 2.7.14). Connecting the opposite long sides of a rectangle with each other makes a tube whereas, in the next step, connecting its opposite short sides closes that tube into a circular form of a torus (Fig. 2.7.11). We can also obtain a torus if we start from two interlocked rings and make one rotate along the other (Fig. 2.7.13, 2.7.15).

The entire surface of a torus is divisible into seven regions, as if paving it into seven tiled areas. By highlighting each one of them with a different colour, it becomes evident that every coloured region touches every other such region only once (Fig. 2.7.14).

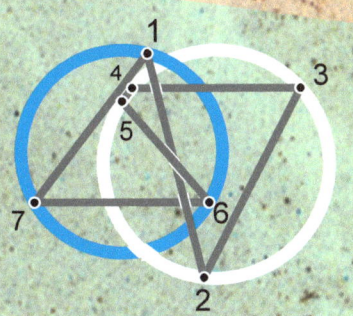

▲ 2.7.13 – *The torus reduced to essentials*

*The
Cell which has
first come into Existence had attained
the Initial Human Form passing through 7 Phases. Only
afterwards had it become dependent on the Order of the All-Dominating and
had been taken into Evolution.*

All Entities and the Entire Creation had gone through 7 Phases until had gotten their present forms. Everything is dependent on the bases of 7 Phases and Evolutions. (Phase, Cellular Form – Evolution, Spiritual Form.)

This is the immutable Principle of the Law of Equilibrium. Everything flourishes in accordance with the Essence-nucleus formula of the Atomic structure.

▲ 2.7.14 – *One of the ways to make a torus is to start from a rectangle*

The Knowledge Book
(F33, p 532, par 4-6)

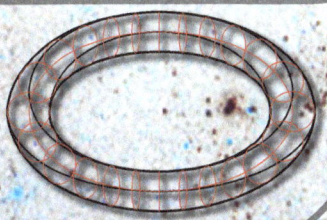

▶ 2.7.15 – *A ring, travelling along another one, produces a torus. Daniel Winter theorises that the torus and the irrational numbers Φ, π and e are the building blocks of a universe.*

2.7.16 – Seven colours are used to map this two-dimensional territory of 19 regions so that each of seven colours touches the remaining six colours only once. The regularity of this perfect touching is emphasised by superimposed circles and triangles. Since the surface of a torus can be paved using seven hexagonal tiles, where each hexagon shares only one side with the hexagon of a different colour, the torus provides a spatial solution to this topological principle.

In the branch of mathematics known as topology, this is often called the *seven colour map* of the torus which complies with the rule that, throughout the entire surface, two adjacent territories are represented with different colours. This unusual property of the torus shape provides a high level of interconnections and communication along its surface area. Thus as an informational database, the torus seems to be an efficient solution.

The more complex topological analysis of seven points, or a complete graph on seven nodes each belonging to one of the seven hexagons that a torus can be tiled with, reveals the existence of a pattern of a trefoil knot on the torus (Fig. 2.7.13, 2.7.17; 2.3.8). It is a tripartite spatial figure that hosts the seven colours, since it goes through each of the seven-colour territories of the torus.

FLOWER SYSTEM

Gürz crystal is an *atomic whole*, floating in the *Thought Ocean of the Pre-Eminent Power*, and it is a focal point of the Total[II-7.4]. One of the three natural dimensions of the *Gürz crystal* is called the *Dimension of Nothingness* and the one in charge of it is the *All-Mighty*. Within this dimension is the so-called *Light-Universe*.

The *Light-Universe* is a receiving and projecting universe which collects the Essence-Power energy of the *Thought Ocean* and projects it onto the *Main Existential Dimension*. The innermost section of the *Light-Universe* is called the *Totality of Central Suns*, and that is the *Dimension of the All-Merciful*, the supervisor of the entire *Gürz crystal*.

The collecting style of energy within the *Light-Universe* is called *flower system*. The flower is made of six energy balls, of the condensed energy collected from the *Thought Ocean*, which the six light-pyramids converge into the big central light-pyramid with the help of the *Technological Dimension* (Fig. 2.7.19). This big light-pyramid then projects the entire power of the *Light-Universe*, as the *Mighty Energy*, onto the *Main Existential Dimension*.

2.7.17 – Is an eye of a torus – the eye of a universe or the Eye of God?

▲ 2.7.18 – Nested toruses

I extended everywhere, in accordance with what was to come into existence, I bent right around myself. I was encircled in my coils; one who made a place for himself in the midst of his coils.

Iru-To, cosmic serpent (coffin text from writing in an ancient Egyptian pyramid)

Black is the real face of the Light. — Nikola Tesla[II-7.5]

The normal form of the seven Light-Universes

The condensed form of the Energies of the seven Light-Universes

From the *Second Universe*, the second natural dimension of the *Gürz crystal*, the *Mighty Energy Focal Point* then projects all the energy it receives from the *Light-Universe* onto the *Reality of the Unified Humanity*, positioned in the third natural dimension of the *Gürz crystal* called the *Dimension of Allness*.

The *Dimension of Allness*, in charge of which is the *All-Dominating*, is like an existential skein made up of 1800 *mini atomic wholes*. Each *mini atomic whole* is a smaller existential skein – that is, one existential dimension. Inside each *mini atomic whole*, 1000 out of 1800 universes rotate anticlockwise and constitute a *centrifugal universe*. The *mini atomic whole* itself is also considered to be a centrifugal universe. The totality made of 1800 centrifugal universes is a backbone of the *Gürz System*.

The *main centrifugal universe* is a nucleus universe composed of 1000 universes and is situated just under the *Main Existential Dimension*. This totality is called the *Reality of the Unified Humanity*, or *ONE*. It projects the operational ordinance of the *Gürz System* onto the *Dimension of Allness* while directly connected to the *Dimension of the All-Merciful*. Its symbol is the six-pointed star, made of two overlapping triangles. This star represents so-called *flower system* (❁ or ⟁).

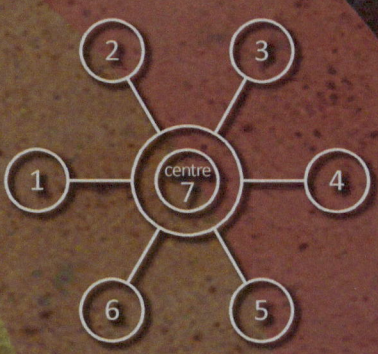

▲ 2.7.19 – *The Knotting and Unification style of the Energies. This scheme from The Knowledge Book*[II-7.6] *confirms the intuitiveness of alchemists, who highly regarded the symbol known as the perfect seal*

From this brief encounter with the *Gürz crystal* we can discover the number 7, as the formation called the *perfect seal* (Fig. 2.7.9, 2.7.10), in the energy unification style of the *Light-Universe* (Fig. 2.7.19) and in the operational ordinance of the *Gürz System* (sextuple system) concealed in the symbol of the *Reality of the Unified Humanity*.

▲ 2.7.20 – *The unification of the 49 colours gives the colour black to Space*[II-9.3]

◀ 2.7.21 – *Momentum in symmetrically opposing directions creates stability/matter/Maya* – Daniel Winter

Love is a Foundation of the entire Ordinance of Cosmoses. Nature and the Human being are also a product of this Love. The Vibration of Love is the Essence source of the Atomic structure. In fact, in every Existing thing there are Vibrations of Love in accordance with their attraction Power. And this is a Natural Vibration.

Vedia Bülent (Önsü) Çorak
(Light)

The Wormhole Centre that bridges the Worlds s your Heart – Jain[II-7.7]

ELEVEN

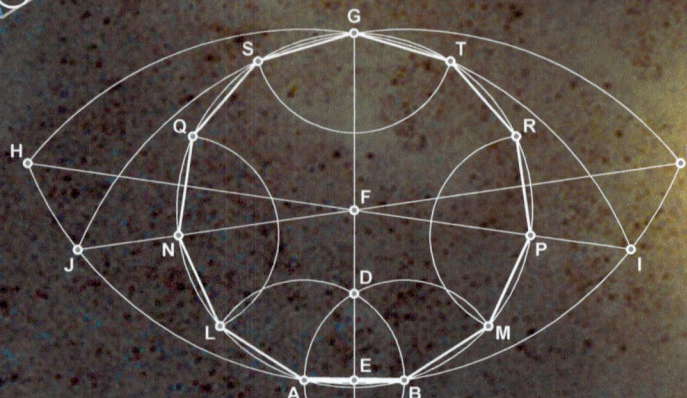

▲ 2.11.1 – Number 11, placed in the group with 7 and 13, within the first 13 natural numbers

◀ 2.11.2 – Symmetrical figures featuring number Eleven

▼ 2.11.3 – Construction of a regular eleven sided polygon

GOD AND ME

The number Eleven is the simplest and the smallest so-called *master number*. The recurrence of digits in *master numbers* stands for the balanced repetition of events, and for patterns in life that are viable in multiple realities.

As we have seen, the number Ten represents a higher expression of the number One, and may serve as a metaphor for the higher self. Since it can be represented as 10+1, the number Eleven symbolises the coexistence of the higher self and the self on equal terms. From a certain point on our life-journey, we start travelling with a constant awareness of God thus experiencing Him inside us and everywhere outside of us. That is the way we live the light of the profound truth of our being. Number Eleven holds a memory of the reunion between God and Me.

Ourselves, our life medium, as well as all Creation, can be seen as a consciousness programme of the Supreme Power coded by numbers and expressed through geometry. Holding the primeval existential secrets, numbers can also work as unique tools which ring the bell of our divine origin and purpose.

The combination 11:11 is considered the symbol of a wake-up call for humanity. It is credited with the ability to trigger some dormant codes in us, to remind us of our divine essence and of our mission on this planet.

11:11 is also associated with some higher laws of existence. The knowledge of it came through the **Altar-Keeper** and **Chief Golden Eagle** – **Mitakuye Oyasin**(II-11.1), an American Indian from the Ihanktowan Dakota Nation (Sioux). **Golden Eagle** was approached by the American, **Dr Richard Boyls**(II-11.2) who was looking for clarification of the photos he made. The photos contained the symbols etched into the body structure of the star-craft that crashed at Roswell in 1947. After consulting spiritual guides from the stars, **Golden Eagle** learned that the photographed symbols represented *Eleven Universal* and *Eleven Spiritual Laws* (Fig. 2.11.4). These laws are accepted by all member civilizations of the Star Nations as a common cultural foundation.

How would you like to peel that onion of duality around you and expose your spiritual core? Do you laugh when you're alone? Is there joy when you're alone? If the answer is no, then you haven't discovered who is there! For if you truly knew about the core, the unity, the angel inside, you might be astonished to realize t is a child! Angels never grow up, you know. They're always one age – youthful, joyful, playful, laughing, and smiling. That's who's in there. That's the one who can create unity on the planet. How about you with you?

Kryon(II-11.3) *(through Lee Carroll)*

You are subject to such a System that only Love, Tolerance, and Goodwill can reinforce the Potential of Your Universe.

The Knowledge Book (F10, p 147, article 52)

Eleven is the master number that reflects the transformation of the physical into the Divine.

Patricia Cota-Robles(II-11.4)

UNIVERSAL LAWS of		SPIRITUAL LAW of
Free Will		Freedom of Man
Change		Growth of Man
Movement and Balance		Strength, Health, Happiness
Innocence, Truth and Family		Protection of Family
Symmetry		Equality
Life		Choice
Light, Sound and Vibration		Intuition
Judgment		Karma
Nature		Protection of Man
Love		Healing
Perception		Future Sight

▲ *2.11.4 – Eleven Universal and Eleven Spiritual Laws and their symbols*

THIRTEEN

▲ 2.13.1 – Number 13, placed in the group with 7 and 11, within the first 13 natural numbers

▼ 2.13.2 – Thirteen bouncing inside the circle

▶ 2.13.3 – An endless line which defines thirteen areas

WIPING AWAY THE OLD

In ancient times, the number Twelve was considered a number of completion and, as such, the herald of a new beginning due to the natural self-exhaustion of some processes. The emerging need of thorough transformation is lived through the number Thirteen which carries the power of wiping away the old and allowing the new to be born organically from within. The number Thirteen is a number of freedom and individuality, also associated with certain cosmic rhythms.

There are thirteen full moons and tide changes within one year. In some cultures such as those of the Celts and Native Americans that followed the lunar calendar of thirteen months in a year, Thirteen was the number of zodiac signs.

The geometrical figure called the *fruit of life* is made of thirteen circles and is a base for the construction of the series of archetypal geometric shapes known as the *Platonic solids*.

There is evidence that the total number of protons in every amino acid is divisible either by Seven, Eleven or Thirteen.

CAPITAL LETTER B

According to *The Knowledge Book*, the uppercase letter *B*, as a graphical symbiosis of the numbers One and Three (B – I3), is the symbol of the number Thirteen[II-13.1]. The number One in it represents the *Pre-Eminent Power* while the number Three stands for the trinity *Lord – All-Merciful – All-Compassionate* which is an administrative totality of the *Gürz crystal*.

The frequency power of each letter is equivalent to its meaning and its dimensional frequency. Since the number Thirteen is an indivisible total and an unchanging symbol of the Lord, the letter *B*, with the number Thirteen concealed in it, carries an extremely intense frequency and the energy power of the dimensions it represents. Those with physical constitutions not accustomed to strong energies, and those in a fearful state, may be affected by them and hence interpret them in a negative way. The *terrestrial consciousness* of some cultures therefore regards the number Thirteen as an ominous number. The root of this belief goes back to an early European myth, but not until after the 17th century has this number acquired an unlucky attribute in the West.

Perception and consideration of the number Thirteen differs around the world. In the ancient cultures of Mexico, Thirteen was a symbol of the Sun and male energy, while the Chinese saw it as a number of difficulties. In the second *Book of Moses*, thirteen attributes are given to God. In India, Thirteen is not considered an unlucky number and neither is it in the Jewish *Kabala*.

Interestingly, the numerical value of the words *love* and *one* in the Hebrew alphanumerical system is Thirteen (Fig. 2.13.5).

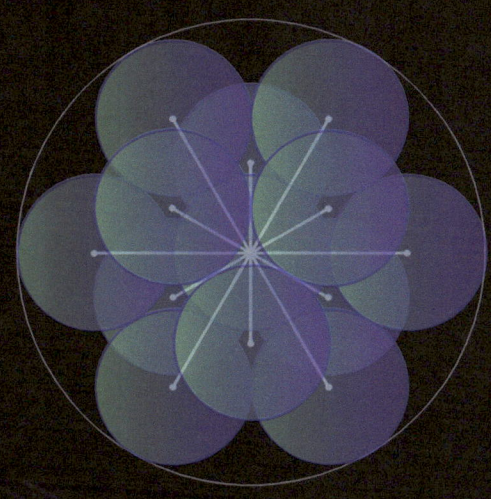

▲ 2.13.4 – In the closest packing of equal spheres, there are 12 spheres that touch and completely surround a central sphere. The centres of these 12 spheres, as vertices, determine a 3D figure called a cube-octahedron (vector equilibrium).
We may add another symmetrical layer of identical spheres, to surround the original 1+12 spheres, according to the same packing rule. This second layer totals 42 spheres while for the third layer, applied in the same manner, we would need 92 spheres.
The number of spheres in all three layers, including the central sphere, is 147 (1+12+42+92).
Interestingly: 147=3x49; 49=7x7

What energy do you carry around that is inappropriate? You know what I speak of, don't you? What won't you release that separates you from love? What energy will you hang on to and hang on to and hang on to? You will not have unity in your own heart or your own biology until that old energy contract is dismissed. It takes two to write a contract, you know. Sometimes it's you and you!

Kryon (through Lee Carroll)

ENTERING THROUGH ALPHA EXITING THROUGH OMEGA

The lower case letter *b* conceals two other numbers connected to the number Thirteen, according to the information from *The Knowledge Book*[II-13.1]. They are the numbers Six and Nine. The number Nine is represented by the right-side-up triangle, and is a symbol of the *Training Religious Dimension*. In it, humans are accustomed to praying and asking God for what they want.

The number Six is obtained by turning the number Nine upside down and consequently is represented with a downward-pointing triangle. It symbolises a universal transition, a *Conveying Dimension* and the *All-Merciful*. In the evolution of that dimension we learn the truth by experiencing the opposite of what we expect and want. We are exposed to the necessary tests until we begin to equally appreciate all our personal experiences and blamelessly accept everything that comes our way. When that happens, we demonstrate an alignment of our individual will, and ego, with the Will of God. Thereafter we see perfection everywhere and serve joyfully on the path of God.

In the context of the lower case letter *b*, the number Fifteen, as the sum of the numbers Six and Nine, stands for the 15th solar system, or the 18th evolutionary dimension that is the entrance to *Omega*. Omega is a layer of consciousness and evolution pertaining to the 19th evolutionary dimension (the 76th energy dimension). The 76th dimension also conceals the number Thirteen (7+6=13). On Earth, the human consciousness starts its evolution at the 3rd evolutionary dimension, marked as *Alpha*. Omega is the final gate we are meant to pass through, treading our path on this planet all the way from the *Alpha entrance*. Hints about this evolutionary objective are given in sacred books and carried through numerous artworks inspired by the words of the Lord God: *I am the **Alpha** and the **Omega**...* (Fig.2.13.6).

...The Biblical relation Be Love – Number 13 is simply incontrovertible.

This profound and inextricable relation between the Number 13 and the concepts of Love and Unity further manifests in the chapter structure of I Corinthians. Without any controversy whatsoever, I Corinthians 13 has been universally recognized as the premier statement of Love to be found in all the Bible, (or anywhere else, for that matter!). It is the uncontested Love Chapter of the Bible – 13 verses in the 13th chapter, with the last verse explicitly structured upon the patter of One and Three! There are endless echoes from the Triune nature of God – Three Divine Persons united as One in perfect Love! Glory to God in the highest!

Richard Amiel McGough

The symbolism of the letter *B(b)*, and the Greek letters *alpha* and *omega,* broadens our view on the meaning and the energy power of the letter/number relationship and at the same time reveals the path of evolution that the supreme realm has intended for us.

הבהא	(Love)	13
דחא	(Unity)	13
דרול	(The LORD)	13x2=26
דחא אוה דרול	(The LORD is One)	13x3=39

▲ 2.13.5 – Alphanumerical analysis of Hebrew words by Richard Amiel McGough

On that day, we will fold the heaven,
like the folding of a book.
Just as we initiated the first creation,
we will repeat it.
This is our promise;
we will certainly carry it out.

The Quran (21:104)

In the Evolutionary scale of Your
Planet, ALPHA is the Entrance,
OMEGA is the Exit. In the selection of
this Medium, first,
there is a Mass Preparation, later,
there is the Individual entrance
to this Dimension.

The Knowledge Book
(F38, p 638, par 8)

◄ 2.13.6 – Christ Pantocrator, Hilandar monastery on Mount Athos in Greece

I am the Alpha and the Omega, says the Lord God,
who is and who was and who is to come, the Almighty.

The Bible (Revelation 1:8)

ENDNOTES

ALL IS NUMBER

I-1   **Johannes Kepler** (1571-1630), German astronomer and mathematician from the time of the Holy Roman Empire. Influenced by Copernican teachings, he formulated three great laws of planetary motions, known as *Kepler's laws*, which describe the revolutions of the planets around the Sun. He worked as court mathematician to the Holy Roman Emperor Rudolf II. Wrote *Misterium Cosmographicum* (1596) and *Astronomia Nova* (1609). He proclaimed astrology a true science, and believed that certain harmonious configurations of planets influence human impulses. In 1724, the Russian empress Catharina the Great bought his manuscripts and deposited them in the observatory of Pulkovo, near St. Petersburg.

I-2   **Pythagoras** (Πυθαγορας, 569BC-475BC) was a Greek philosopher who made important contributions to mathematics, astronomy and the theory of music. He was born on the island of Samos, off the coast of Asia Minor, and lived for 22 years in Egypt, 12 years in Babylon and probably spent some time in India prior to settling in Croton (presently Crotone in Southern Italy) where he established a of philosophy modelled on a secret society.

I-3   **Mohammed Mustafa** (570-632), an Islamic prophet whose name means *Most Praiseworthy*. As the Messenger of Allah, he brought light to mankind in the last sacred book revealed to this planet. At the age of forty, he received his first revelation through the Archangel Jibril (Gabriel); and messages from Allah, *The One True God*, continued for the following 23 years until the end of his life. Mohammed dictated these messages to others who wrote them down. The collection of these writings was named *The Quran* – a book sent to both Humankind and Jinns (beings created from a smokeless fire that existed before the creation of Adam). The collection of Mohammed's personal thoughts is known as the *Hadith*.

I-4   **Galileo Galilei** (1564-1642) was an Italian physicist and philosopher, considered the father of modern astronomy, modern physics and generally the first modern scientist. His contributions to science include, amongst numerous others, the use of mathematics in experimental physics, improvements to the telescope, putting forward the first and second laws of motion and the first principles of relativity. He supported Copernicus by believing in the heliocentric model of the solar system.

I-5   **Lao Tzu** (老子, 570BC-490BC – though many believe he never existed), was born in Ch'u (the present-day Henan Province in China). Lao Tzu literally means *Old Master*. He was a contemporary of Confucius in China as well as of Plato and Socrates in Greece, and Buddha in India. Lao Tzu is the founder of *Taoism*.

I-6   **Philolaus** (Φιλόλαος, c480BC-c405BC) was an ancient Greek mathematician and philosopher, a contemporary of Socrates and Democritus, and an immediate pupil of Pythagoras. He was the first to publish a book on Pythagorean teachings. He pioneered the doctrine of the Earth's revolving around the Sun, and suggested a circular form for the Earth's orbit. He also supposed the Sun to be a disk-like reflector of light coming from the universe and calculated the lunar month as 29½ days, the lunar year as 354 days, and the solar year as 365½ days.

I-7   *The Knowledge Book*, given through Vedia Bülent (Önsü) Çorak, contains the frequencies of all sacred books, revealed to our planet so far, together with the frequency of the *Mighty Energy Focal Point*. It is a *Universal Constitution of the Lordly order* also called the *Golden Book of the Golden Age* or the *Book of Truth*. All references relate to hardcover book (Second Edition, January 1998); www.dkb-mevlana.org.tr

I-8   **Dr Rashad Khalifa** (1935-1990) was an Egyptian scientist with a PhD in biochemistry. He was the first to put the Arabic text of *The Quran* into a computer and to analyse its words and letters, particularly its mysterious initials. Dr Khalifa was the first Arabic native speaker to translate *The*

Quran from his mother tongue into English. In 1974 he claimed a discovery of the mathematical miracle of *The Quran* based on the number 19; www.submission.org

I-9   **Richard Amiel McGough**, holds a BSc in Mathematics and Physics from *Washington State University* (1985), and studied Quantum Physics while working on his PhD. He is an expert Web developer, Visual Basic 6.0 developer, ActiveX developer and Microsoft Certified Professional. McGough is the sole author and designer of the BibleWheel.com website. He also published the book: *THE BIBLE WHEEL – A Revelation of the Divine Unity of the Holy Bible*. Both the website and the book are a comprehensive study of *The Bible*, both in Hebrew and Greek, that reveals the numerical base of this sacred book's structural excellence. The website has an astonishing online database with 2335 interlocked identities. It presents a coherent scientific model of *The Bible* as a divinely designed *Wheel of God* attributed with perfect sevenfold symmetry; www.biblewheel.com

I-10   **The alphanumerical tables** of the Arabic, Greek and Hebrew alphabets:

	ARABIC			GREEK			HEBREW		
sequential value	numeric value	letter	name	numeric value	letter	name	numeric value	letter	name
1	1	ا	Alef	1	Α, α	Alpha	1	א	Alef
2	2	ب	Beh	2	Β, β	Beta	2	ב	Bet
3	3	ج	Jeem	3	Γ, γ	Gamma	3	ג	Gimel
4	4	د	Dal	4	Δ, δ	Delta	4	ד	Dalet
5	5	ه	Heh	5	Ε, ε	Epsilon	5	ה	He
6	6	و	Waw	7	Ζ, ζ	Zeta	6	ו	Vav
7	7	ز	Zain	8	Η, η	Eta	7	ז	Zayin
8	8	ح	Hah	9	Θ, θ	Theta	8	ח	Het
9	9	ط	Tah	10	Ι, ι	Iota	9	ט	Tet
10	10	ي	Yeh	20	Κ, κ	Kappa	10	י	Yod
11	20	ك	Kaf	30	Λ, λ	Lambda	20	כ	Kaf
12	30	ل	Lam	40	Μ, μ	Mu	30	ל	Lamed
13	40	م	Meem	50	Ν, ν	Nu	40	מ	Mem
14	50	ن	Noon	60	Ξ, ξ	Xi	50	נ	Nun
15	60	س	Seen	70	Ο, ο	Omicron	60	ס	Samekh
16	70	ع	Ain	80	Π, π	Pi	70	ע	Ayin
17	80	ف	Feh	100	Ρ, ρ	Rho	80	פ	Pe
18	90	ص	Sad	200	Σ, ς	Sigma	90	צ	Tsadi
19	100	ق	Qaf	300	Τ, τ	Tau	100	ק	Qof
20	200	ر	Reh	400	Υ, υ	Upsilon	200	ר	Resh
21	300	ش	Sheen	500	Φ, φ	Phi	300	ש	Shin
22	400	ت	The	600	Χ, χ	Chi	400	ת	Tav
23	500	ث	Theh	700	Ψ, ψ	Psi	500	ך	f. Kaf
24	600	خ	Khah	800	Ω, ω	Omega	600	ם	f. Mem
25	700	ذ	Thal				700	ן	f. Nun
26	800	ض	Dad				800	ף	f. Pe
27	900	ظ	Zah				900	ץ	f. Tsadi
28	1000	غ	Ghain						

I-11   **Gillian MacBeth-Louthan** is a clairvoyant psychic, a metaphysical teacher, messenger and internationally known medium. For over 35 years she has been working with the *Councils of Light, Mary Magdalene, Merlin, White Buffalo Calf Woman, Mother Mary, Pleiadians* and many other energies of the Christ Light; www.thequantumawakening.com

I-12   **Confucius** (孔夫子, 551BC-479BC) was an ancient Chinese thinker who claimed to be a *transmitter who invented nothing*. His name translated from Chinese means *Master Kong* (Kong Fuzi or K'ung-fu-tzu). His philosophy was collected and published posthumously, in the *Analects*.

THIRTEEN STORIES

ONE

II-1.1   All attempts by the author to reveal the originator, and to contact the originator/guardian of this figure, have been to no avail. The same applies to the illustrations featured in figures: 2.1.2, 2.2.3, 2.4.14, 2.8.9, 2.7.7, 2.13.6 then *The Last Supper* by Leonardo da Vinci (pages 61-62), and the image of the Archangel Michael on the page 75. If you have information about them, please contact the author via the publishers in order to give proper acknowledgement.

II-1.2   **Mevlana Celaleddin-i Rumi** (1207-1273) worldwide celebrated poet and Sufi mystic. Just like Zoroaster, he was born in the Persian city of Balkh (present-day North Afghanistan). A 3000-year-history makes Balkh one of the oldest cities in the world. Many cultures left their mark on it: Buddhists, Greeks with Alexander the Great, Arabs, and Mongols with Genghis Khan. Escaping from the Mongols in 1225, Rumi's father settled with his family in the city of Konya in Anatolia (Turkey), then part of the Turkish Seljuk Empire. Rumi was the founder of the Mevlevi Sufi order, a mystical brotherhood of Islam. His most famous work is a poetical interpretation of themes from *The Quran*, in the Pahlavi language, known as the *Mesnevi*.

II-1.3   **Thoth**, mythical immortal ruler and sage of ancient Egypt, was credited with the transfer of all knowledge and hieroglyphic writing to Egyptians. The ancient Greeks believed him to be the architect of the *Great Pyramid* and compared him with their own God Hermes, adding the attribute *Trismegistus (Trice-great)* to his name to make a distinction. The books assigned to the divine messenger Thoth are known as *Hermetica*, and are Africa's contribution to the treasure of ancient wisdom – the same as *Upanishads, Tao Te Ching and Dhammapada* are contributions from the Far East.

II-1.4   **Yael** and **Doug Powell**, *Messages from God;* www.circleoflight.net

II-1.5   *Gürz – natural Gürz crystal;* explained in the book *Cosmic Diagrams*, chapter FRACTALS

II-1.6   **Ibrahim F. Karim**, PhD, Egyptian architect, the father of the new science of BioGeometry™. With Rawya Karim, MA, he founded the *BioGeometrical Systems Institute Company* in 1993 as a design centre for research and implementation of BioGeometry™. More information about their work in the book *Messages behind Shapes;* www.biogeometry.com

II-1.7   **Milena**, Chinese colours on rice paper (detail); www.milena.org.uk

II-1.8   *Tantra*, a spiritual discipline, originates from ancient Indian religions. It is generally focused on harmonising the female and male energies with the goal of achieving enlightenment. The tantra path includes a thorough exploration of life through a variety of practices, like *yantra, mantra*, identification with deities, taboo breaking, concentration on the body, self-analysing and cleansing the self of negative thoughts. Tantric tradition also involves developing the skills needed for the transformation of sexual energy for the purpose of spiritual advancement.

TWO

II-2.1 Seng Ts'an (520-606) was an ancient Chinese sage, the third patriarch of Zen Buddhism in China.

II-2.2 Noel Huntley, PhD, English scientist with a background in physics and doctorates in psychology and parapsychology, also a talented painter and musician, with a keen interest in computers. He has developed the foundation for a spiritual science as well as for the physics of a higher dimensional consciousness. Some of his books are: *ET and ALIENS: Who Are They? And Why Are They Here?; The Scientific Principles of Spiritual Enslavement* and *Attainment of Superior Physical Abilities and the New Science of Body Motion.* His website *Beyond Duality* is a collection of articles on variety of topics, like evolution, the nature of time, ascension, consciousness, holographic civilisation, fractals, types of physics and the theory of one; www.users.globalnet.co.uk/~noelh

II-2.3 Rabia Al Basri (717-801), a poetess and mystic born in Basra (present-day Iraq) known for introducing the concept of Divine Love: loving God not out of fear but for God's own sake.

II-2.4 About reaching the *Will of the Total*, see Vedia Bülent (Önsü) Çorak, *The Knowledge Book*, Fascicule 30, pages 478-480 and 484-485

II-2.5 Ronna Herman is an internationally known lecturer and author of eight books. The books and messages transmitted to her from Archangel Michael have been translated into most major languages and read around the world. You may contact her at: RonnaStar@earthlink.net, www.ronnastar.com

II-2.6 Vedia Bülent (Önsü) Çorak, *The Knowledge Book,* Supplement 5, page 1058

II-2.7 Daniel Winter, a writer and lecturer in the areas of electrical engineering, psychophysiology (the origin of languages), computer animation in multimedia and non-linear energy source technologies. Winter developed superior technology for measuring coherent emotions in the heart *(HeartTuner*, also called *BlissTuner).* In his research and practical work he bridges the physical with the metaphysical; www.fractalfield.com

FOUR

II-4.1 From the lecture given by Beinsa Douno on August 13th, 1937, The Rila Mountain. Bulgarian-born Peter Constantinov Deunov (1864-1944) is also known by his spiritual name Beinsa Douno. He was a spiritual teacher and the founder of a school of Esoteric Christianity; www.beinsa-douno.com

II-4.2 Image from Rob Krier's book *Architectural Composition*, used with the kind permission of the Papadakis Publishers

II-4.3 More on colours of *Omega dimension* and the *Alpha channel* in *The Knowledge Book*, Vedia Bülent (Önsü) Çorak, Fascicule 54, page 950

II-4.4 Ahmes was the Egyptian scribe who wrote *The Rhind Papyrus* (1832 BC). It is one of the oldest known mathematical documents, which illustrates Egyptian knowledge of mathematics and its application in the areas of engineering, money counting and the calendar. As a text book for mathematician-priests, *The Rhind Papyrus* reveals their theoretical skills in geometry and algebra. The Greeks who visited Egypt, and studied at their temples, spread that knowledge – for example Thales of Miletus who introduced the study of geometry into Greece. Thales also advised Pythagoras to visit Egypt.

II-4.5 Archimedes (Αρχιμήδης, 287 BC-212 BC), Sicilian, Syracuse-born ancient Greek mathematician and inventor considered to be one of the greatest mathematicians ever. He is most famous for discovering the hydrostatic principles of density and buoyancy while stepping into a bathtub.

The story says that in his excitement he ran into the street naked, crying *Eureka! (I have found it!)*. His mathematical achievements were outstanding for his time. He perfected the method for integration and was able to find the surface area and volume of many bodies. He also defined the existence of a constant in relation to the circle, later known as π (Pi), which he calculated as 3+10/71~3.1408 and 3+1/7~3.1429. Archimedes introduced mechanical curves and calculated the oldest known geometric series. Some of his inventions are: the hydraulic screw for raising water, the catapult, the burning mirror, the lever and the compound pulley.

II-4.6 Plato's Academy was built in 428BC, in Athens, on a site continuously inhabited since prehistoric times. The philosophical school gained fame thanks to the Neoplatonists. It existed for more than seven centuries, before Emperor Justinian closed it in the year 347AD.

II-4.7 Johann Heinrich Lambert (1728-1777), a German mathematician, in 1761 was the first to prove that the number π (Pi) is an *irrational number*. 33 years later, the French mathematician Adrien-Marie Legendre (1752-1833) also proved the irrationality of π, while in 1882 another German mathematician, Ferdinand von Lindemann (1852-1939), proved π to be a *transcendental number*. Lindemann's result meant that the ancient mathematical puzzle *squaring the circle* (constructing a square, with a compass and ruler, the area of which equals that of a given circle) – was impossible to solve.

II-4.8 Vedia Bülent (Önsü) Çorak, *The Knowledge Book*, Fascicule 3, page 37; Fascicule 34, page 547

II-4.9 Karl Gustav Jung (1875-1961) was the Swiss psychiatrist and founder of analytical psychology who, in his early career, collaborated with Sigmund Freud. His broad interests included philosophy of both the West and the East, sociology, religion, astrology, mythology, art, literature, alchemy and dreams. Jung coined terms, used in analytical psychology, such as: *archetype, synchronicity, collective unconscious, psychological complex,* the *Anima* and the *Animus*.

II-4.10 Drunvalo Malchizedek, the originator and the teacher of the *flower of life* programme and *Mer-Ka-Ba* meditation; www.spiritofmaat.com; www.drunvalo.net

EIGHT

II-8.1 Nikola Tesla (1856-1943) was an inventor, electrical and an mechanical engineer, a physicist, and a visionary of profound genius devoted to science and peace. The father of the radio and modern electrical transmission systems, he is often regarded as one of the greatest scientists in the history of technology. Tesla was born to Serbian parents in the Austro-Hungarian Empire (present-day Croatia) where he spent his childhood. The last 56 years of his life Tesla spent in the USA, where he patented 700 inventions. Among them are the alternating current induction motor, Tesla-coils used in radio and television sets, fluorescent lights, wireless communications and the transmission of electrical energy, vertical take-off aircraft, the laser beam, and remote controls and robotics. The use of solar energy and the power of the sea were some of his visions.

II-8.2 More about the operational order of spiral vibrations in *The Knowledge Book,* Vedia Bülent (Önsü) Çorak, Fascicule 34, pages 556-558

II-8.3 Reflection of evolutionary dimensions (based on information from *The Knowledge Book*, Vedia Bülent (Önsü) Çorak, Fascicule 44, pages 739-744) – illustration, Milena

II-8.4 Chemical elements are substances composed of atoms that cannot be reduced by ordinary chemical methods. All matter is composed of them. The *periodic table* is an arrangement in columns (groups or families) and rows (periods) of the chemical elements, ordered by their atomic number (number of protons within the atomic nucleus) which emphasises the periodicity of their properties.

II-8.5 Fengshui is more than 3000 years old a Chinese practice, for the proper arrangement of space, that originates from Taoism. Traditional *fengshui* addresses the planning of buildings, villages and cities in such way that harmony with the environment and seasonal changes is achieved. The resulting design is meant to bring peace, good health, wealth and good fortune.

II-8.6 The Yoruba are the largest ethnic group in Nigeria who also live in other African countries, like Benin, Togo, Sierra Leone, as well as in Cuba and Brazil on the American continent.

II-8.7 One of the *16 Pieces collection*; courtesy of Olalekan Babalola, the founder and the director of *Ifa-Yoruba Contemporary Arts Trust;* www.ifayorubacontemporaryarts.co.uk

II-8.8 Vedia Bülent (Önsü) Çorak, *The Knowledge Book,* Fascicule 24, pages 364-365

II-8.9 Book *Ascended Master Instruction* (Saint Germain, Series Vol. 4)

THREE

II-3.1 Vedia Bülent (Önsü) Çorak, *The Knowledge Book*, Supplement 6, page 1064

II-3.2 Sheldan Nidle is a representative and lecturer for the *Galactic Federation of Light*. He founded the *Planetary Activation Organization (PAO)* in November 1997; www.paoweb.com

II-3.3 Vedia Bülent (Önsü) Çorak, *The Knowledge Book*, Fascicule 30, pages 482-484 and 486

SIX

II-6.1 Vedia Bülent (Önsü) Çorak, *The Knowledge Book*, Fascicule 24, page 364; Fascicule 37, page 618

II-6.2 Wilson Bentley (1865-1931) – illustration from *The Annual Summary,* taken from *The Monthly Weather Review* for 1902. Bentley was a farmer whose hobby was photography, and he photographed more than 5000 snowflakes.

II-6.3 Illustration by Reschetnayak, courtesy of Mr. Kjell R. Björklund (Norway).

II-6.4 Acantharia are marine protozoa related to *Radiolaria*. They contain an organic capsule which surrounds a central mass of cytoplasm.

II-6.5 Vedia Bülent (Önsü) Çorak, *The Knowledge Book,* Fascicule 52, pages 902-903

NINE

II-9.1 Gautama Buddha was named Siddhārtha Gautama at birth and lived in ancient India between c563BC-c483BC. He was a spiritual teacher and the historical founder of Buddhism. In a general sense, the word *Buddha* can be used for anyone who becomes enlightened by spiritual cultivation – the purification of the body and mind, the discovery of the true nature of reality, the transcendence of suffering, and the practicing of a moral life through the virtues of the *middle path* and the *noble eightfold path. The Dhammapada*, the wisdom of Gautama Buddha consisting of 423 verses in Pali, was recorded some four centuries after Buddha lived.

II-9.2 Vedia Bülent (Önsü) Çorak, *The Knowledge Book*, Fascicule 2, page 21

II-9.3 For more about the significance of the number 147 and its connection to the number 13, see *The Knowledge Book*, Vedia Bülent (Önsü) Çorak; Fascicule 16, pages 242-244

II-9.4 Illustration based on the work from Michael S. Schneider's book *A Beginner's Guide to Constructing the Universe – the Mathematical Archetypes of Nature, Art, and Science*; www.

constructingtheuniverse.com

II-9.5   Nicomachus of Gerasa (c60-c120) was a mathematician born in Roman Syria (present-day Jordan). He was a Pythagorean who wrote *The Introduction to Arithmetic* – the only surviving document on the Greek number theory. With his other book, *The Manual of Harmonics*, he furthered the Roman knowledge of proportion previously described by Theon of Smyrna. Later on, with the works of Leon Battista Alberti, Andrea Palladio and Le Corbusier *(Modulor)*, the general theory of proportion was shaped.

II-9.6   Vedia Bülent (Önsü) Çorak, *The Knowledge Book*, Supplement 5 , pages 1054-1056

II-9.7   Vedia Bülent (Önsü) Çorak, *The Knowledge Book*, Fascicule 29, pages 458-462

II-9.8   From the book The Wellspring of Good: *The Last Words of the Master Peter Deunov* compiled by Bojan Boev and Boris Nikolov, pages 136-138

FIVE

II-5.1   Vedia Bülent (Önsü) Çorak, *The Knowledge Book*, Fascicule 24, pages 364-365

II-5.2   See the book *Golden Proportion*; section *Golden family*

II-5.3   Mikhael Ivanov (1900-1986), a Bulgarian philosopher, pedagogue, alchemist, astrologer and mystic. Inspired by fellow Bulgarian spiritual master Peter Deunov, he moved to France in 1937 to spread the teaching of the Universal White Brotherhood and to save it from communism. On his visit to India (1958-1960), Maharaja Nimcaroli Babaji gave him the name Omraam Mikhaël Aïvanhov. Aïvanhov travelled extensively throughout the world giving conferences. His philosophy and teachings, based on Christianity, are recorded in numerous books and tapes in which he explores ways for man to better understand his own self in order to grow and acquire perfection. Aïvanhov was a master who lived what he preached.

II-5.4   Based on the information from *The Knowledge Book* by Vedia Bülent (Önsü) Çorak – illustration, Milena. More about colours and evolutionary scales in Fascicule 34, pages 559-560; more about the 5th dimension – Karena in the Fascicule 16 (pages 231-234), Fascicule 22 (pages 335-339) and in the Fascicule 29 (pages 458-463); more about the *KU* and *RAN* frequencies in the Fascicule 36, pages 601-603; Leonardo da Vinci – *Vitruvius Man,* with blue and orange pentagons added by Milena.

TEN

II-10.1   For more information on the *tetraktys* see chapter *ALL IS NUMBER*

II-10.2   Iamblichus (c250-c330) was a neoplatonic philosopher born in Syria

SEVEN

II-7.1   Vedia Bülent (Önsü) Çorak, *The Knowledge Book*, Fascicule 54, page 947

II-7.2   Vedia Bülent (Önsü) Çorak, *The Knowledge Book*, Fascicule 29, pages 458-463

II-7.3   Vedia Bülent (Önsü) Çorak, *The Knowledge Book*, Fascicule 36, pages 603-605

II-7.4   Information based on *The Knowledge Book*, Vedia Bülent (Önsü) Çorak; Fascicule 35, pages 564-577. More about the *Gürz crystal* in the Fascicule 53, pages 931-933.

II-7.5   **From the theatre play Tesla or accommodation of an Angel**, by Stevan Pešić, National Theatre Belgrade Publication.

II-7.6   **Illustration** from *The Knowledge Book*, Vedia Bülent (Önsü) Çorak, Fascicule 35, page 565

II-7.7   **Jain**, born in Australia to Lebanese parents, is the author of 12 books and 6 DVDs on ancient knowledge in the areas of *Vedic mathematics, magic squares, sacred geometry, divine proportion* and the *Platonic solids*. As a theatrical director he developed a maths enrichment programme for schools called *MatheMagics*. Through a performance called *The Theatre of the Holy Numbers*, mathematics is taught through a play in which actors wear elaborate costumes. Jain has been lecturing in schools and universities around Australia for more than 15 years. He authored many exhibitions on mathematical art, and is also a healer/herbalist and muralist; www.jainmathemagics.com

ELEVEN

II-11.1   **Mitakuye Oyasin** – Standing Elk/Golden Eagle Chief/Chief Black Spotted Horse; www.star-knowledge.net

II-11.2   **Dr Richard Boylan** PhD, MSW, MS, Ed, BA, is an internationally-noted researcher of UFOs/star visitors and human star kids/star seed adults, a Behavioural Scientist, Exo-Anthropologist, emeritus University Associate Professor of Psychology, registered Social Worker and certified Clinical Hypnotherapist; www.drboylan.com (The illustration 2.11.4 used by his kind permission.)

II-11.3   **Kryon** – Magnetic entity, channelled through Lee Carroll; www.kryon.com

II-11.4   **Patricia Cota-Robles** is one of the founders (in 1980) of *The New Age Study of Humanity's Purpose, Inc.*, an educational non-profit organisation; www.1spirit.com/eraofpeace

THIRTEEN

II-13.1   **Vedia Bülent (Önsü) Çorak**, *The Knowledge Book*, Fascicule 36, pages 606-608

Front cover: Detail of the *Dimension of the All-Truthful*
Graphic design of the book: zodrag@gmail.com

BIBLIOGRAPHY

- ANTI-GRAVITY & THE WORLD GRID, edited by David Hatcher Childress; Adventures Unlimited Press
- THE ANCIENT SECRETS OF THE FLOWER OF LIFE, Volume 1 & 2 by Drunvalo Melchizedek; Sedona Color Graphics
- A BEGINNER'S GUIDE TO CONSTRUCTING THE UNIVERSE – The mathematical archetypes of Nature, Art, and Science a voyage from 1 to 10 by Michael S. Schneider; Harper Perennial, a division of Harper Collins Publishers
- CELTIC SPIRALS – handbook by Sheila Sturrock; Guild of Master Craftsman Publication Ltd
- FENG SHUI – The Traditional Oriental Way to Enhance Your Life by Stephen Skinner; Siena book, an imprint of Parragon
- THE FRACTAL GEOMETRY OF NATURE by Benoit B. Mandelbrot; W. H. Freeman and Company, New York
- THE GEOMETRY OF ART AND LIFE by Matila Ghyka; Dover Publications, inc. New York
- HIDDEN NATURE – The Startling Insights of Viktor Schauberger by Alick Bartholomew; Floris Books
- THE IMPLOSIONS' GRAND ATTRACTOR – Sacred Geometry & Coherent Emotion; assembled, Edited & Distributed from Daniel Winter's writing by Implosion Group
- ISLAMIC PATTERNS – An Analytical and Cosmological Approach by Keith Critchlow; Thames and Hudson, London
- JUST SIX NUMBERS – The Deep Forces that Shape the Universe by Martin Rees; Weidenfeld & Nicolson – London
- THE KNOWLEDGE BOOK – Messages received and transformed into writing by Vedia Bülent (Önsü) Çorak; World Brotherhood Union Mevlana Supreme Foundation, Istanbul
- L' ASTROLOGIE SACRE – Miroir de la Grande Tradition, Frederic Lionel; Editions du Rocher, Monaco
- LET THE NUMBERS GUIDE YOU – The Spiritual Science of Numerology by Shiv Charan Singh; O Books, Winchester, UK; New York, USA
- MAGIC SYMBOLS by Frederick Goodman; Brian Trodd Publishing House Limited
- THE MASTER MASONS OF CHARTRES by John James; West Grinstead Publishing
- NATURE'S NUMBERS – Discovering Order And Pattern In The Universe by Ian Stewart; Weidenfeld & Nicolson – London
- NUMEROLOGY with Tantra, Ayurveda, and Astrology – A Key to Human Behaviour by Harish Johari; Destiny Books, Rochester, Vermont
- ORDER IN SPACE – A Design Source Book by Keith Critchlow; Thames and Hudson, London
- PATTERN AND DESIGN WITH DYNAMIC SYMMETRY – How to Create Art Deco Geometrical Design by Edward B. Edwards; Dover Publications, inc, New York
- RANDOMNESS by Deborah J. Bennett; Harvard University Press, Cambridge, Massachusetts, London England
- SACRED GEOMETRY by Miranda Lundy; Wooden Books Ltd
- SACRED GEOMETRY – Philosophy and practice by Robert Lawlor; Thames and Hudson
- SECRETS OF ANCIENT AND SACRED PLACES – The world's Mysterious Heritage by Paul Devereux; Brockhampton Press, London
- SUNLIGHT ON WATER – A Manual for Soul-full Living – The One With No Names through Flo Aeveia Magdalena
- SYMMETRY IN CHAOS – A Search for Pattern in mathematics, Art and Nature by Michael Field and Martin Golubitsky; Oxford University Press
- THE JOY OF PI by David Plather; Bath Press Colourbooks, Glasgow
- THE SECRET SCIENCE OF ECSTASY AND IMMORTALITY – IMPLOSION by Daniel Winter
- THE TRUE POWER OF WATER – Healing And Discovering Ourselves by Masaru Emoto; Beyond Words Publishing, Inc., Hillsboro, Oregon
- YANTRA – The Tantric Symbol of Cosmic Unity by Madhu Khanna; Thames and Hudson

Copyright © Milena 2015
All rights reserved.

No part of this publication may be reproduced, stored in or introduced into a retrieval system, or transmitted, in any form, or by any means (electronic, mechanical, photocopying, recording, or otherwise) without the prior written permission of the copyright owner.

Published by
M PUBLISHING
www.memento13.com

A catalogue record for this book is available from the British Library

ISBN
978-1-909323-03-2

www.ingramcontent.com/pod-product-compliance
Lightning Source LLC
Chambersburg PA
CBHW040057160426
43192CB00002B/100